The Right-Wing Threat to Democracy

The Right-Wing Threat to Democracy

The Undoing of America's Exceptionalism

BURT HALL

iUniverse, Inc.
Bloomington

The Right-Wing Threat to Democracy
The Undoing of America's Exceptionalism

iUniverse books may be ordered through booksellers or by contacting:

iUniverse
1663 Liberty Drive
Bloomington, IN 47403
www.iuniverse.com
1-800-Authors (1-800-288-4677)

ISBN: 978-1-4759-2696-5 (sc)
ISBN: 978-1-4759-2697-2 (hc)
ISBN: 978-1-4759-2699-6 (e)

Library of Congress Control Number: 2012908525

Printed in the United States of America

iUniverse rev. date: 06/25/2012

To My Lovely Wife Lynn

Table of Contents

Highlights

———·•·———

This book shows how flaws in our system of government are being exploited to gain and misuse power, and how this is contributing to our nation's decline. It lays out clearly what these basic flaws are and how they can be fixed. If elected officials do not act, the American people have alternatives.

During the twentieth century, America's exceptionalism remained unquestioned. Since the beginning of the twenty-first century, there has been a sharp decline in the well-being of its citizens. We have suffered serious reversals and cannot afford another decade like it.

While both parties struggle constantly for political advantage, the right wing has excelled at it by exploiting weaknesses in our democracy and using political conspiracies to gain control of government. Painful consequences have followed. These consequences are discussed throughout the book and are so enormous and long term that only future historians can fully assess their impact.

If you find all of this hard to believe, set aside your initial impressions and continue reading. The highlights that follow will give you a preview of the entire book and a roadmap to each of eight chapters where full documentation can be found.

Rejection of the People's Choice of President

The right-wing's quest for power began in a big way during the era of President Clinton when it refused to accept his two elections and declared war on his two administrations.

Right-wing leaders launched a series of lengthy but baseless congressional investigations of the President and the First Lady and replaced a highly reputable Independent Counsel with an inexperienced one who became their designated point man to bring down the Presidency. The investigations turned up nothing but were not terminated until President Clinton left office.

In a lengthy conspiracy to bring down his Presidency, the right-wing: (1) manipulated our judiciary system to convert a sexual slander suit against one of its own magazines to an unwarranted sexual harassment suit against the President, (2) used that suit to set up a perjury trap, (3) convinced the U.S. Supreme Court to allow this disruptive civil suit to go forward on a sitting president, (4) used false information to mislead the Justice Department into authorizing a conflict of interest investigation and (5) broke two federal laws in the process.

Right-wing House leaders knew the Senate would not convict the President. Their mission was to force him to resign from office and take back the White House in the next election. To accomplish this they railroaded the President's impeachment in a lame duck House session and used blackmail to get the necessary votes.

Four hundred historians and 430 law professors tried to reason with House right-wing leaders against violating their constitutional responsibilities. However, obsessed with regaining the White House, they listened to no one including the American people, who had just rejected impeachment by voting a stunning Republican setback at midterm elections.

By putting an undeserved mark of impeachment on a man's place in history, right-wing leaders dishonored themselves, the House Judiciary Committee, the House of Representatives, and the U.S. Constitution.

Three House leaders later resigned in disgrace, and two key players who drove the impeachment process acknowledged regret. But, the right wing did accomplish its mission – a transfer of government power back to its own party (See chapter one).

The improper transfer of power disrupted what had been the nation's top priorities at the time: (1) balancing federal budgets and (2) dismantling the al-Qaeda network which had already declared war against the United States and made several attacks.

Now in Charge, the Right Wing administration Does Not Respond to Extraordinary Warnings of 9/11 Attacks

The administration of George W. Bush had been fully informed by President Clinton, the CIA Director, and other top experts of the gravity of the threat to our nation posed by the al-Qaeda terrorist network.

Then, during the following spring and summer, the Bush administration received numerous warnings of the upcoming 9/11 attacks from friendly countries and three heads of state—Prime Minister Blair of England, President Putin of Russia, and the King of Jordan.

Some of these warnings specified how the attacks, directed by al-Qaeda leader Osama Bin Laden, would occur and the presence of al-Qaeda members here in the U.S. planning the attacks and learning how to fly.

When the warnings had reached a crescendo about two months before the attacks, the CIA Director made an emergency visit to the White House. He presented a compelling case for military action at that very moment. None was taken, not even precautions to protect our commercial aircraft.

Both the White House and investigative 9/11 Commission successfully covered-up this breach of national security (See chapter two).

Ironically, the breach in security created a major crisis which would soon be exploited politically by the Bush administration to sell a war in Iraq, gain full control of Congress, and obtain a second term. The campaign slogan was "Stay Safe: Reelect Bush." The consequences of 9/11 were enormous:

- Untold financial damage to the United States and a huge loss of precious human life,
- Bin Laden's elevation to a world hero among Muslims and the attraction of many recruits to his cause,
- A worldwide increase in terrorism, and
- Unnecessary wars that have caused a huge drain on our national resources even to this day.

Immediately after the 9/11 catastrophe, the right-wing administration executed a plan passed on by the Clinton administration to remove the al-Qaeda network from Afghanistan, but allowed Bin Laden, to escape. This debacle was followed by a failed terrorism policy and two needless wars.

Launching Two Needless Wars

The failure to respond to the repeated 9/11 warnings led to a war-like mentality and right-wing leaders lashed out against terrorism in an irresponsible way.

In the case of Afghanistan, a military invasion and occupation were totally unnecessary and represented a misjudgment of enormous proportions. All that was required was a surgical military/CIA operation to take down Bin Laden and his al-Qaeda network, as had been proposed during transition by the previous administration (See chapter two).

Our presence there could have ended long ago with unmistakable warnings of what would happen to the people of Afghanistan and their government if they ever again allowed a safe haven for a terrorist network intent on attacking the United States. In fact, fear of severe retaliation caused that country's foreign minister to warn us of the 9/11 attacks two months before they occurred.

The war in Iraq was never really justified by the facts. To support that war, the right-wing administration used selective intelligence known to be inherently uncertain as absolute fact. They created an imagined linkage to 9/11 and dramatized all of this information to frighten Congress and the American people. We were victims of a public relations campaign.

Findings of international inspectors inside Iraq were already discounting U.S. intelligence and easily could have prevented war. The U.S. invasion, however, stopped the inspectors from completing their work and forced them to leave prematurely.

Under the War Powers Act, it is easy to start wars but extremely difficult to stop them. The right wing has abused the authority to go to war. Congress needs to reform that Act to deter future war adventures of this kind and require public hearings on alternatives to war, alternatives to military occupation, and if war is authorized, alternatives to an exit strategy (See chapter three).

Resulting Decline in U.S. Foreign Policy and National Security

Right-wing policies during its two terms in office began a sharp decline in U.S. foreign policy, national security, and superpower status. World opinion of the United States changed from great admiration to almost universal dislike and distrust.

Wars are not the answer to organized, mobile terrorist networks. They do not address the threat aimed at undermining governments across the globe and killing innocent civilians. Using the right of self defense, our military responses ought to be surgical in nature, using elite Special Forces in *any* country that allows a safe haven for terror networks to attack us.

It has never been U.S. policy to use wars to remake cultures in distant lands. We have enough problems with our democracy here at home. The two right-wing wars will ultimately cost the nation at least four trillion dollars without having improved our national security. When authorizing any future wars, the Executive Branch and Congress need to broaden the public debate by:

- Reinstituting the draft (temporarily) to ensure shared sacrifice across our society and sufficient manpower to carry them out,
- Raising taxes so that future generations will not have to pay for them, and
- Developing a new policy to confront international terrorism that removes the fortress mentality we have today. Such a policy is outlined in chapter four.

Other matters giving rise to a decline in our international standing and an exploding federal debt are the right–wing administration's mishandling of such issues as a defensive missile shield, space weaponry and nuclear disarmament.

U.S. President John F. Kennedy led the way toward control of nuclear weapons so they would not end the world as we know it. Over decades, many countries have become concerned over the slow progress of the larger powers in responding to a nuclear disarmament treaty. Some have joined the nuclear club themselves by acquiring nuclear weapons. Others simply remain frustrated.

The two recent right-wing administrations did not make progress in outlawing the use of nuclear weapons and now, two recalcitrant regimes—neither a free democracy—are threatening to add their names to the nuclear club.

The U.S. should seriously reexamine the value of nuclear weapons in today's world and work with the international community on a treaty to dismantle them worldwide as *unlawful*. Like biological weapons, their use should be made unthinkable. (See chapter four).

Passing on a Nation in Decline

The right-wing left the next administration with two misguided wars, a failing terrorism policy, monstrous deficits, a jobless economy in crisis, a tumbling stock market, and urgent domestic problems, including:

- Continued U.S. enslavement to Mideast oil,
- A rapidly growing threat of climate change,
- Under regulated financial institutions,
- A devastated housing market,
- A broken health-care system, and
- A decaying educational system.

Even before the next president took office, analysts predicted that the new president would be stuck with dramatically rising commitments and would spend his entire four years trying to figure out how to accommodate the long-range costs of the previous administration's policies.

During its eight-year reign, the right wing structured a spiraling national debt into future budgets. Their leaders voted repeatedly to raise the federal debt limit, eventually by some $4 trillion, while at the same time making ill-advised tax cuts.

The combination of doubling our national debt, two costly wars, a severely depressed economy, and escalating deficits created dire consequences of an unknown magnitude for the next president. As an economist advised a member of Congress, there was no alternative but to "keep the financial system from going into cataclysmic default."

During the transition to a new administration and soon afterwards, the economy lost over four million jobs. With an economic meltdown deeper than anyone had anticipated, falling tax revenues, and the absence of private capital, the new president was in the unenviable position of having to further raise the federal debt in order to:

- Stabilize the financial system,
- Assist both small and large businesses in distress and, in particular, the auto industry,
- Wind down responsibly the two wars he inherited,
- Provide unemployment insurance and food stamps to those in dire need, and
- Start satisfying long-ignored domestic needs such as developing new sources of energy.

Allowing our federal debt to go even higher, right-wing holdovers in Congress blocked creation of a congressional commission to reduce annual deficits. They blocked this commission as soon as they discovered the new President supported it.

The same congressional leaders then refused to support recommendations of a presidentially created deficit-reducing commission, although its proposals were highly regarded by members of both parties. The standoff over raising the debt ceiling that followed disrupted government and lowered our nation's credit rating.

Excessive right-wing reliance on oil as a source of energy has weakened our national security and allowed competitors in other nations, like China, to get a head start on producing electrical energy with new technologies invented here.

The right-wing's unyielding denial of generally accepted scientific evidence on climate change threatens our ailing planet. Their leaders in Congress have repeatedly stalled solutions to protect the world we live in. A group of teenagers have finally filed lawsuits to compel the government to take action. They want to clean up this mess and protect future generations. (See chapter five).

A Second Rejection of the People's Choice of President

After suffering a major defeat at the ballot box and handing over a nation in decline, right wing leaders chose not to work with President Obama and forced his party to govern alone. Ruthless obstruction returned big time. A new record was set for stalling tactics and filibustering in Congress. The end result was a partial and unproductive governing body in Congress with the lowest approval rating in history.

Desperate to regain power it had just lost, the right wing resurrected the McCarthyism era, smearing the new president with harsh terms, questioning his patriotism, and accusing him of not being an American citizen. Their extremist behavior has demonstrated little respect for our democratic process and institutions.

The right-wing propaganda machine repeatedly pounds misinformation into the minds of the less informed until they finally begin to believe it. Research shows that highly partisan people rarely change their minds because their belief system dictates which facts they choose to accept.

After the right-wing took control of the House in 2011, its leaders directed national attention to deficit reduction and women's rights rather than to jobs and economic growth. Because people generally vote with their wallets, keeping the economy in low gear offers an easy path for a right-wing victory in the 2012 election. It is a desperate strategy to gain power, but the dangers of buying into it are clear:

- During its previous eight-year reign, the right wing had the worst track record of job creation since the government began keeping records after World War II—despite huge tax cuts and the stimulus of two unending wars.
- The right-wing tendency is not to invest in our crumbling infrastructure, industries of the future, or education of our workforce.
- The right wing will undo progress made by the current administration as it did after the two Clinton administrations (See chapters two through five).
- Recovery from a national crisis is not the right time to revert back to the party that caused it (See chapter six).

Repairing Our System of Democracy

According to an NBC News/Wall Street Journal survey in November 2011, most Americans believe we are "at the start of a longer-term decline where the U.S. is no longer the leading country in the world."

If our vital institutions of democracy—Congress, the media, and the Supreme Court—had done their jobs, the circumstances we face today would be entirely different. As will be seen, the outcome of two presidential elections would have been different, the 9/11 catastrophe and the two wars that followed could have been avoided, and there would be no spiraling national debt to contend with.

As previously stated, the Supreme Court blundered when it allowed a politically conspired and unfounded sexual harassment case to go forward against a sitting President. The Court did this on the absurd grounds that it would *not* be a distraction to the Clinton presidency. Instead, the case gave the right-wing the one thing it was desperate for—a media frenzy with a road to the White House.

The Supreme Court's decision violated our constitutional right to have presidents devote full time and attention to running the country and not be hamstrung by civil suits. The case itself was dismissed. The plaintiff has since acknowledged that she was being used by people with a political agenda (See chapter one).

The media frenzy that followed allowed the right wing to gain control of the White House, but not without the help of a second, misguided U.S. Supreme Court decision. The Court barred a Florida vote recount from proceeding, and the presidential candidate who lost the vote count was awarded the election. Had the Supreme Court not interfered for the first time in history with a state's right to have its votes counted, the Bush administration would never have come to power. (See chapter seven).

There certainly would have been no war with Iraq if the Supreme Court had not simply handed the presidency to a right-wing administration. President Bush was not forthcoming with the American people on the Iraq War and our only lines of defense were Congress and the media. Neither came to our rescue.

Congress did not delve deeply into the intelligence issue or insist that the international inspectors in Iraq be allowed to finish their job. Had it done so, there would have been no war.

If Congress had called in the Joint Chief of Staff's top intelligence official, Major General Glen Shaffer, it would have gotten a good picture of the great uncertainty and lack of evidence surrounding the alleged weapons of mass destruction. That official had already shared his views with the Secretary of Defense, but they were not acted on.

Much of the media had more interest in getting imbedded with U.S. forces and reporting from the war zone than with challenging the war itself. Several major media publications have since acknowledged publicly that they fell down on the job (See chapter seven).

A second term of the failed Bush right-wing administration could easily have been avoided and two needless wars terminated had the 9/11 investigative commission simply revealed the White House's grave breach of national security during the months preceding the attacks (See chapter two).

Rather than a Bush reelection campaign, a different Republican candidate would have had to run for office with a different agenda and a different outcome.

The media nibbled around the edges for years with thousands of articles on the 9/11 catastrophe, but management never authorized an enterprising journalist to pull together all of the bits and pieces and tell the full story with the depth and breadth it deserved.

Some of the questions reporters should have found answers to were (1) why did the president obstruct the 9/11 investigation, (2) why did he resist its creation in the first place, and (3) why was his critical role and that of his national security team missing from the 9/11 Commission report?

All the evidence was out there, including the warnings which were so carefully documented in a book by Paul Thompson called *Terror Timeline: Year by Year, Day by Day, Minute by Minute: A Comprehensive Chronicle of the Road to 9/11.* It showed the fever pitch of the many credible and specific warnings that had been around for months.

Compelling revelations were also in several articles and in a book on Cheney's Vice-Presidency authored by a Pulitzer Prize winning journalist.

And, Bob Woodward's book, *State of Denial*, should have tipped off any discerning media person to a paralyzed White House national security apparatus.

A film still on the Internet (*9/11 Press for Truth*) includes an outright confession by 9/11 Commissioner Bob Kerrey on what actually happened during the Commission's deliberations and his views on the President's negligence.

The 9/11 Commission staff director had a serious conflict of interest. He had worked with the administration then under investigation and had co-authored a book with the President's National Security Advisor Condoleezza Rice. Following his 9/11 Commission duties he became her Counselor at the State Department. Where was the media's curiosity?

We now have a media dominated by a few corporations that are more concerned with their bottom lines and their relationships with key government officials than with keeping the public well informed. Regarding 9/11, the question must be asked: Does the mainstream media have the ability to confront a sitting President on a matter of life and death accountability?

Two media professionals, who have studied Washington politics and Congress for over 40 years, have concluded that the core of the problem in our democracy rests with (1) a Republican Party that has moved too far from the mainstream and (2) a media that distorts reality by hiding behind the refuge of balanced reporting. Public hearings are sorely needed into the overall conduct of the media in our democracy (See chapter seven).

Increasing Shift of Political Power to the Wealthy

Wealthy individuals and corporations have disproportionate influence over public policy because of the often decisive role that money plays in our political system and the government decisions that follow.

For several decades, the tax burden of the wealthiest Americans has been dramatically lowered, and their income has soared. Their reduced taxes have left them more money to influence politicians and the decisions they make. Aside from direct contributions, they pour big money into Super PACs organized to influence the outcome of elections. In return, they manage to keep or gain further tax reductions, loopholes, subsidies, and tax havens.

Big corporations have found imaginative ways to dodge their taxes and obtain huge refunds. The *effective* tax rates of corporations fell to a forty-year low of twelve percent in 2011. More than 50,000 millionaires are paying lower taxes than millions of middle class income taxpayers.

Patriotic Millionaires for Fiscal Strength and two other similar groups are saying "let the Bush tax cuts for the wealthy expire once and for all." They argue the wealthy job creator argument is a myth (See appendixes V and VI).

The loss in tax revenue strains government budgets, cuts public services, and causes other taxpayers to absorb the shortfall. It increases our interest payments on the national debt.

Corporations and the wealthy, not the average person, are the ones who benefit the most from huge government investments in infrastructure, education, safe and efficient transportation, new technologies, scientific research, and national security. The inventions of the Internet and space miniaturization of electronics are but two examples of how private industry has received enormous benefits from long-term government investments.

Two authors of a 2012 book, Why Nations Fail, warn that economic inequality translates into political inequality and the concentration of power in the hands of only a few. A group of the very wealthy could ultimately control the economic and political life of our entire nation. Famous Supreme Court Justice Louis Brandeis warned, "You can have wealth concentrated at the top, or democracy, but you cannot have both."

We need to stop debating tax rates that are a mere fiction, reform and simplify the tax code, outlaw corporate tax havens, and increase the *effective* rate for corporations and high income people. (See chapter seven).

Overhauling Our Electoral System

Chapter seven also raises the issue of whether our system of electing presidents and candidates to office is under siege and whether future elections will reflect the will of the people.

The idea behind our democracy is that we can influence government by observing what our legislators do and then refuse to reelect them, if they do not abide by the people's will. Citizen participation cannot be achieved if big money interests and its lobbyists in Washington are allowed to influence election outcomes and the government decisions that follow.

A true democracy depends on putting a stop to the purchase of political officials either directly or indirectly through election financing. Our country decided long ago that corporations should not be allowed to buy elections, but a right-wing leaning Supreme Court has reversed that long-established precedent with its Citizens United decision.

The Court decided that corporations have a First Amendment right of free speech to spend from their treasuries to influence elections and run attack ads against candidates of their choosing.

Chapter seven includes a lengthy analysis of that decision and its flaws. The flaws apply not only to the decision itself, but also to those who made the decision. Much of the analysis is based on the Court's monumental dissent and three excellent articles dissecting the decision and how to reverse it (See also next section on Legitimacy of U.S. Supreme Court Decisions).

The right wing has decided that a larger electorate is not in its best interest. It has initiated widespread voter suppression and barriers to a citizen's right to vote. The voting rights of many millions are threatened, as is the future of our democracy.

The targets are the usual suspects: the young, people of color, the disabled, the elderly, and low-income people. Battleground and other Republican-controlled states are involved. The co-director of the Advancement Project in Washington referred to this right-wing strategy as "the most significant setback to voting rights in a century."

This effort at voter suppression includes restrictions on voter registration drives, elimination of same day registration, restrictive photo identification laws and cutbacks on early and absentee voting. Whether currently illegal or not, these laws hinder voting rights. Women are more vulnerable than men because of marital status changes in names and addresses.

If these efforts succeed, there could well be another improper transfer of government power, as happened in year 2000.

What we have in our democracy today is a large number of safe seats in Congress and in state houses across the country because the districts represented are purposely drawn to favor the party in power and/or the incumbent.

In addition, a relatively small number of party officials and voters in primaries determine the public's choice of candidates running for office. As a result, there are fewer truly competitive races and the distinct possibility that extremists, rather than more representative or moderate candidates, will be elected to office.

This longtime trend is connected to the increasing shift of the Republican Party to the extreme right and helps to explain why its moderates have practically vanished. The resulting gap in philosophy of the two major parties in Congress makes it difficult, if not impossible, to find common ground and reach compromises on matters of vital importance to the American people. Major electoral reforms are needed to:

- Get big money corruption out of politics by having taxpayers invest in their own democracy with partial public financing and caps on private donations,
- Make our electoral system more accessible to candidates seeking office and to all eligible voters,
- Permit more competitive and representative elections based on independently drawn voting districts and open primaries,
- Allow a national popular vote to elect presidents rather than just a few battleground states. (See chapters seven and eight).

Legitimacy of U.S. Supreme Court Decisions

The U.S. Supreme Court is our "court of last resort". It is an unelected third branch of government with extraordinary power and is accountable to no one. The legitimacy of some of its crucial decisions is being questioned because partisan politics have infected right-wing leaning members. No longer can we depend on the Court to render independent and impartial decisions.

The Court has blundered on political matters influencing the outcome of three national elections. Two of these were previously highlighted:

first, allowing a vast right-wing conspiracy to disrupt and undermine a presidency and second, not allowing a state voter recount of the narrowest presidential election in history. Together, they led to an improper transfer of government power.

In a third devastating decision, the Supreme Court opened the doors in the 2010 midterm elections to unlimited and anonymous political contributions from corporations, both domestic and foreign. These big-money interests can now influence elections anywhere in the United States at their choosing, and have already done so.

As previously discussed, the Bush administration should never have been reelected. That reelection, however, made possible the appointment of two right-wing judges to the Supreme Court, one of whom is the chief justice. This, in turn, enabled a close 5-4 decision to reverse century-long precedents and open the flood gates for big money interests to invade our political system.

The ruling has enormous implications. It gives Republicans increased corporate power and a large funding advantage to win presidential elections and opportunity to maintain a right-wing dominated Supreme Court for decades to come. Organizations, called Super PACs, are simply another bank account for candidates. And, now corporations and unions can act as though they are individuals, spending their shareholders' and members' money without their consent or knowledge.

Right-wing members of the court have come under criticism for getting involved in political activities, not stepping away from legal cases in which justices have a conflict of interest, accepting political gifts, and legislating from the bench.

Several groups have called for an investigation and disbarment of one right-wing Supreme Court Justice. In addition, fifty-two members of Congress and 130,000 citizens have demanded that the chief justice investigate him for unethical behavior.

A group of more than 100 lawyers from around the country has asked Congress to require the Supreme Court to adopt an ethical code of conduct, as lower courts do. The code would clarify when one or more of the justices must step away from a legal case because of a conflict of interest. This action is opposed by the chief justice and right- wing leaders in Congress.

Congressional oversight and public pressure forced an earlier Supreme Court Justice to resign for ethical reasons, and this can be done again. Much is needed before we can rely on the Supreme Court as a legitimate third branch of government. With public pressure, Congress needs to:

- End Supreme Court immunity to federal ethics laws and require the Court to establish a process for disqualification of members from cases in which they have a conflict of interest,
- Require Supreme Court judges to discontinue participation in overt political meetings and events,
- Impeach any Justice found guilty of improper conduct, and
- Appoint judges with practical wisdom and stop lifetime appointments if conditions do not improve (See chapter seven).

Repairing Our System of Politics

What has been called "the American century" may come to an end unless we return to our Constitution and representative democracy. This would mean (1) overhauling our electoral system, (2) reorganizing how Congress does business, and (3) keeping the public properly informed so citizens can truly participate in government affairs and make the best possible choices of our national leaders and congressional representatives.

Four political movements—Independent, Americans Elect, No Labels and Occupy Wall Street—are challenging our current system of politics. They have in common restoring power to the people by reducing partisanship and ending big money corruption of our political system. Leaders of the Independent Movement go further. They seek to transform the whole political system by ending political parties and restructuring our political process.

The Independent movement has been gathering momentum over the past two decades. Their position is simple: Our country is faced with monumental challenges, and our partisan political system is not up to the task.

At one time, we had many moderate statesmen in the Republican Party who participated in great debates and were willing to work with presidents of the opposite party. Some made magnificent contributions to our country and became famous for it. Their pictures now decorate the halls of Congress, and two have Senate buildings named after them. In 2012 articles, two remaining Republican moderates challenged the direction of their party. (See appendixes IX and X).

The right-wing views the White House as its birthright. The issue is how far a particular party may go to regain power without crossing the line and doing irreparable damage to our country. Once a party's obsession with power overshadows the public interest, deterioration of the country sets in. That is exactly what has been happening to America.

The right wing uses political conspiracies to retain or regain control of government. New ones are in play for the 2012 election. They include:

- Erecting barriers to voting rights and suppressing Democratic voter turnout,
- Using unlimited sums of money from undisclosed sources to buy elections, and
- Obstructing the President's agenda by trying to substitute its own that was previously rejected at the ballot box.

We have reached the stage in our politics and democracy where an extreme element of one party will not let another one govern successfully. Only the public's voting power and an overhaul of our electoral system will remedy the tendency of political leaders and their supporters to choose power over country.

Power politics is too ingrained in the right wing to expect change absent public pressure and restraint of big money influence on politics. There may be temporary truces when it becomes expedient, but they will not last. The right wing will not break its addiction to power until the public demands it.

A long-time Republican staffer who served in both houses of Congress resigned in 2011 after losing faith in his party. His revelations in chapter eight about his own party are wide-ranging and deeply troubling.

An eight-term former Republican congressman has confirmed what the public already suspects—the current system in Congress is unworkable and the "struggle for party advantage trumps all other considerations." He recommends a number of changes in how our Congress operates and in how states nominate and elect candidates for office (See chapter eight).

The future of the Republican Party depends on using more acceptable means to regain power, revising its agenda to appeal to mainstream voters, and allowing moderates to reenter their Party and hold leadership positions. Without moderates, there will continue to be a deficit in Republican leadership.

The politics of self-interest and pursuit of power adversely affect us all. As private citizens, we don't have to accept what has happened over the past two decades. We can change things for the future.

More than one fourth of Americans are not registered to vote. A well-informed public, which uses its right to vote regularly, can prevent power politics from overriding the public interest. A modern system of universal voter registration system and use of partial public financing will remove big money corruption from election financing and increase public interest in voting.

The public's main goal would be to reward and penalize political parties and politicians according to their performance, agenda, political behavior, and respect for our democratic institutions.

Congress must reform itself and the electoral system by drawing on the eight-term Republican congressman's recommendations referred to above and those of others who have served or are now serving in Congress.

The recorded history in the eight chapters that follow is a wake-up call for any thinking American. It's a call to action for all who care enough about our democracy to fight back. Remedies to help fix our system of government can be found in these chapters and are summarized in Appendix IV. If elected officials do not act, the American people can take matters into their own hands (See chapter eight).

A final commentary concerns John F. Kennedy and how the end of his short, but extraordinary presidency relates to what has happened over the past two decades and what is happening today.

"This is not a battle between Republicans and Democrats ... it is between the ultra right wing element, who want to mold us in their image only, and those of us who want to preserve an open, free nation for our children and grandchildren."

A former investment executive and moderate
Republican, now an Independent

Chapter One

REJECTION OF PEOPLE'S CHOICE OF PRESIDENT

"We are an endangered species . . . my wing of the party has been swept into oblivion by the ultra right, which now controls the Republican agenda."

A former moderate Republican

The right wing of the Republican Party decides what it wants to do and then pursues a win-at-any-cost strategy to achieve its ends. Right wing adherents assume they have a "divine" right to govern and a right to tear down those who don't share their beliefs.

During the two Clinton administrations, they tried every means at their disposal—unethical, illegal and unconstitutional—to undermine his administrations and force resignation. Subversive politics disrupted the presidency and eased the way for the right-wing takeover of the White House in 2001. It all started with –

Refusal to Accept Presidential Election Results

After much campaigning and political infighting, we elect a president every four years. These elections provide legitimacy to a new or continued administration. Traditionally, Americans pull together and support the elected president. That tradition was broken in the 1990's.

Republicans owned the White House for twelve years before Clinton's election and were outraged at the loss of the presidency. Clinton was seen as a usurper, his victory illegitimate and he had to be driven from the White House. To accomplish this, he had to be brought down.

In the aftermath of Clinton's election, right wing members of the business legal and church communities, and the political establishment collectively mounted covert and other efforts to disable the President's administration and remove him from office. Their tentacles spread far and wide. Some of the key players were:

- Investment bankers Peter Smith and Richard Mellon Scaife, both of whom paid huge sums to finance any possible scandal—no matter how farfetched. Scaife is believed to have spent from $200 to $300 million trying to influence government policy and "steer this country to his brand of hard-core conservatism." He financed a right wing magazine, *American Spectator,* whose role was to trash the President, without much regard for the facts, and drive him from office.[1]

- Lawyers Richard Porter, member of the first Bush administration, and Ted Olson, a member of both Bush administrations. They were actively involved behind the scenes, playing important roles in various assaults on the President. Olson participated in several Scaife-funded activities and was intent on undermining the Clinton presidency without disclosing his own involvement.[2]

- Jerry Falwell and Pat Robertson who represented the opposition from the religious right. Falwell's organization, Moral Majority, promoted videotapes accusing the President of drug-dealing and the murder of White House aide, Vince Foster—among other things.[3]

- A group from Arkansas who stood ready and willing to feed the right wing network. They included political opponents who were financial opportunists and incensed over Clinton's success. The "Arkansas Project," sponsored by Scaife, was a four-year, $2.4

million attempt to gather information "leading to political ruin of the President."[4]

- Newt Gingrich, who became the new right-wing Speaker of the House in 1994. Gingrich called the Clinton administration "the enemy of normal Americans" and said in a private meeting he would use "subpoena power" to wage war against the White House. He envisioned as many as twenty congressional investigations being conducted simultaneously.[5] Smith and Scaife were both major contributors to Gingrich's campaigns and causes.[6]

Gingrich would later try to use a government shut-down to force an unacceptable budget on the President. According to an eight-term Republican congressman who served with Gingrich (See chapter eight), Gingrich changed the way Congress did business by polarizing his party and being constantly at war with Democrats. He and his Majority Whip, Tom DeLay were the architects of partisanship and the politics of personal destruction.

- Tom DeLay, House Majority Whip from 1995 to 2003. He diverted the nation and Congress itself from confronting the ongoing menace of international terrorism by using extraordinary measures to force through the House of Representatives an illegitimate impeachment of the President.[7]

These facts, and those which follow, are just a small part of a vast right wing conspiracy documented by highly reputable journalists in these books: (1) The Hunting of the President, (2) A Vast Conspiracy, (3) Blinded by the Right, (4) The Breach: Inside the Impeachment and Trial of William Jefferson Clinton and (5) The Clinton Wars.

Plot to Create Unwarranted Sexual Harassment Suit and Manipulate U.S. Judicial System

The Paula Jones incident first surfaced in an American Spectator article by journalist David Brock in January, 1994—two years after President Clinton was elected to office. In that article, Brock wrote about a sexual encounter by the then Governor Clinton of an Arkansas and a state employee, Paula Jones.

Brock later expressed regret for having written it and confessed to using innuendo and unverified charges to spice up his material. He received $5,000 from investment banker Peter Smith to begin researching the article. Brock found out later that Peter Smith had paid another $30,000 to sources of Brock's article (known in the trade as "cash for trash").[8]

Richard Porter formed a group of lawyers to support and advise Paula Jones.[9] Rather than sue *American Spectator* Magazine for its distortions, her advisors decided to advance their own agenda by working covertly to manipulate the courts in a sexual harassment suit against the President. Referred to as the "elves," the advisors kept their participation a secret from even their own law firms.[10]

Richard Porter's law partner Kenneth Starr offered to work free for Jones. He had six telephone conversations with Jones' group of lawyers, in which he offered *his* opinion that presidents were not immune from civil suits. He stated publicly several times that the suit should proceed without delay.[10a]

Scaife donated $50,000 to help Jones sue the President. A member of Gingrich's House staff would be her chief fundraiser. People close to the case, which was filed on May 6, 1994, suspected that anything that happened between the two principals was consensual, but they pursued it to humiliate the President and hasten his destruction.

The plan was to set a perjury trap when the case came to court by interrogating the President about any past relationships when he was then Governor of Arkansas.[11]

Reputable Independent Counsel Secretly Replaced by Ken Starr to Destabilize the Clinton Presidency

That same year, following right wing demands for inquiry into a failed Arkansas Whitewater land deal that occurred in the 1980's, Attorney General Janet Reno appointed Robert Fiske as Independent Counsel to investigate Whitewater, as well as the President and First Lady's involvement.[12] In the next several months, Fiske moved fast, initiating several local prosecutions in Arkansas. Unexpectedly, a three-judge panel replaced him with Ken Starr. They did so after ultra-right Senators, Jesse Helms and Lauch Faircloth, secretly put pressure on the panel.[13]

Fiske had been aggressively pursuing the Whitewater case and had impeccable credentials and a reputation for fairness. Starr, on the other hand, had no investigative experience and opposed Clinton on every major issue of the day. Starr became the "designated point man in a strategy ... to destabilize the Clinton presidency."[14]

Despite his few qualifications, additional investigations were heaped on Starr's plate. They included probes into White House travel office firings, possible misuse of FBI files, and the suicide of White House aide, Vince Foster.[15] Afterwards, Starr went beyond his authorized scope to make numerous inquiries into Clinton's private sex life while Governor of Arkansas.[16]

Eventually, Starr would spend $70 million trying to bring down the Clinton presidency. Other Independent Counsels spent another $40 million investigating members of his Administration. In the end, not one top official was convicted of a public crime.[17]

Empty Handed, Starr Eventually Resigns, But Only Temporarily

Recognizing that any case against the Clintons was over, Starr's best people began leaving his employ. Those who stayed on were "the unemployable and the obsessed."[18] Suddenly, in 1996, Starr announced plans to accept a teaching position at Pepperdine University in California—without closing *any* of his investigations. The new position had been arranged earlier by Scaife, possibly as an incentive.

The right wing and the media were stunned. The Washington press corps had succumbed to allegations of Clinton's wrongdoing, but Starr couldn't prove them. Outraged, columnist William Safire of the *New York Times* newspaper described Starr as "a man with a warped sense of duty" who "had brought shame on the legal profession by walking out on his client—the people of the United States."[19]

Meanwhile, the right wing published a futuristic book, The Impeachment of William Jefferson Clinton. It imagined Clinton's payment of hush money during the Whitewater investigation and his later impeachment. The book had an anonymous author—widely rumored to be Ted Olson—and included a forward from a Congressional right winger, Republican Bob Barr, saying it was, "... required reading for every citizen of this country."[20]

The right wing continued to hope Starr would inflict a mortal wound on the President. This was a theme of Ted Olson's anonymous satire in *American Spectator*. Bombarded by protests and attacks on his reputation, Starr decided to stay on as Independent Council.[21]

High Court Blunders, Allows Civil Suit Against Sitting President

In 1997, the Supreme Court allowed the Jones sexual harassment suit to go forward during the President's term in office on the grounds that it would *not* be a *distraction*! The Dean of American Journalism, David Broder, explained the Court's decision this way:

> *"One of the great blunders of American history ... one of the dumbest decisions in the long history of the Court ...when they decided that a President should have no immunity against civil suits while serving in office, they may have broken their own record for ignoring reality."* [22]

Under our Constitution, once a president assumes office he owes the public his full time and attention. Civil suits can hamstring a sitting president during his entire time in office. During an *NBC* interview, even Paula Jones acknowledged the disruption her suit might create and said she was willing to wait until the President's term was over. However, the Supreme Court placed her case above the public good and disregarded the U.S. Constitution.

Years later, Jones would publicly admit, on the *Larry King Show*, to being used by people with a political agenda.

Starr Sets Up Monica Lewinsky Investigation

The mid-nineties were desperate times for Starr and his men. They had drilled dry holes concerning the Clintons for several years, and their supporters were unhappy. Starr's people had given up on charging the President with any wrongdoing, but they were in no rush to close their cases.[23]

In 1997, a new cast of characters surfaced led by Linda Tripp. A public affairs employee at the Pentagon, who had previously worked in the White House, Tripp had illegally wiretapped her friend and White House intern, Monica Lewinsky talking about her relationship with the President. This was a relationship he might deny if interrogated on the Paula Jones case.[24]

Starr had no authority to intervene, but he moved fast. He went to the Justice Department and begged for more authority on the grounds of a link between the Lewinsky matter and his Whitewater land investigation. The presumed, but fictitious, link in the two cases was the President's friend, Vernon Jordan.[25]

Starr Then Misleads Justice Department into Authorizing Investigation

According to Starr's people, Jordan had given job assistance to Lewinsky in exchange for false testimony she would give for the President in the Jones case, if called upon to testify. Starr's people then pressured Attorney General Reno into a snap, overnight decision, by telling her that *Newsweek* would soon be reporting a sensational sex story and cover up —including any refusal by Reno to let the Independent Counsel investigate.[26] In making their case, Starr's office provided both incomplete and false information.

- *Newsweek's* top echelon actually had decided not to print the Lewinsky sexual affair. It was Reno's overnight approval that eventually tipped the scales in favor of publication.[27]
- Starr's people omitted the important fact that Vernon Jordan had been helping Lewinsky find a job in New York long before she ever got a Jones subpoena. There was never any overlap with the Whitewater land deal.[28]

Starr Fails to Reveal Three Conflicts of Interest

Starr did not disclose his previous involvements in the Jones case. He had had a number of consultations with Paula Jones' lawyers, had advocated her case in public, and had offered to work free for her.[29]

Starr's office said they'd had no contact with the Jones team. Actually, they were already in collusion with Jones' group of legal advisors —the "elves."[30]

Starr did not disclose that his law partner (Porter) was conspiring behind the scenes to undermine the presidency, as well as to set up a perjury trap in the unwarranted Jones suit.[31]

After getting the new investigation, Starr's people then implored *Newsweek* to hold up publication of the sex story until the President had answered the Jones deposition—the long awaited ambush was set.[32]

Attorney General Accepts False Information Without Statutorily Required Review

The Independent Counsel statute was clear. Attorney General Reno had to make a review herself and find "credible evidence" before the statute could be triggered for an investigation. Had she done so, she would have found (1) the suspicions about Vernon Jordan were untrue, (2) there were no grounds for expanding Starr's authority and (3) several conflicts of interest undermined Starr's capacity to do an independent and impartial review.[33]

The problem with Reno's overnight decision is that the Independent Counsel statute does not operate on mere suspicions or hearsay, but on evidence determined to be credible by Justice Department officials themselves. Further, Starr had an axe to grind and was not the right person for the job. Reno pulled the trigger too fast, too soon, and worst of all based on bad information.

Unfortunately, her ill-advised decision triggered a situation impossible to control—the assignment of a sex scandal to a biased team of investigators with an unlimited budget, who were intent on bringing down the President.

A few weeks later, the presiding judge dismissed the Jones lawsuit and concluded that the Lewinsky matter was not material to that case. An appeal was later settled out of court. So, now we have Starr abandoning several unfinished investigations to chase obstruction in a sexual harassment case—and there was no case to obstruct.

Starr Violates His Statute to Advocate Impeachment

As Bob Woodward of the *Washington Post* newspaper reported, Starr's decision to send a massive narrative of the Clinton-Lewinsky sexual relationship to Congress was "pathetic and unwise."[34] To the dismay of many, right wing House leaders made the report immediately available to everyone—including children—in excruciating detail on the Internet.

The history and charter of the Office of Independent Counsel is clear. The Independent Counsel is a prosecutor and fact-giver, not an impeachment advocate for a particular political party in power. Because of Starr's strong advocacy, his ethics adviser, Sam Dash, immediately resigned. Dash said that by acting as the House's "prosecuting counsel for impeachment," Starr had violated the statute requiring him to present evidence but not conclusions.[35]

In late summer 1998, just before release of Starr's report, our country suffered its third terrorist attack. The bombing of two U.S. embassies had killed over 200 people and injured about 5000. At that very time Osama Bin Laden declared war on the United States, saying "to kill the Americans—civilians or military—is an individual duty for every Muslim."[36]

House Leaders Use Blackmail to Railroad Impeachment in Lame Duck Session

Well over two-thirds of the American people favored Clinton remaining in office and made their views known by rendering a huge setback to Republicans during midterm elections in November, 1998. At this juncture, impeachment was for all practical purposes dead.[37]

While Chairman Henry Hyde of the Judiciary committee had earlier promised the American people a fair hearing on the Starr report, the Republican setback in recent mid-term elections reduced its majority in the next Congress to almost nothing.

Instead of a deliberative, bipartisan approach, right wing House leaders moved with all the speed of "The Roadrunner." The lame-duck House called no witnesses, conducted partisan hearings, and had only party-line votes.[38] The President's lawyers had to testify even without knowledge of what the impeachment charges would be.[39]

Ignoring the public's disproval, right-wing leaders drove two impeachment articles through a final House vote in December just days before the people's newly elected Congress would convene. At the last minute, Speaker Bob Livingston reversed himself saying, "We've got to stop this ... this is crazy." He called an emergency meeting of his leadership, stating, "We're going to have a censure vote." But others prevailed on him to continue.[40]

The House action was a rush to judgment never before witnessed on a matter of such profound importance. At the outset, the House Judiciary committee said it would establish standards to guide the impeachment process. These standards were never set and this paved the way for disregard of our Constitution.

A few moderate Republicans refused to go along. Several others *immediately* regretted their vote and said so publicly—but it was too late.[41]

Two decades earlier, House impeachment proceedings had led to President Nixon's resignation from office for abuses of power and misconduct in office. The House's impeachment of Nixon depended on three things: (1) factually-based hearings with witnesses, (2) bipartisan cooperation, and (3) statesmanship. All three of these were conspicuously missing during the House impeachment of President Clinton.

The Right-Wing's Real Mission – Force the President to Resign

As documented in Peter Baker's The Breach, powerful Majority Whip, Tom DeLay, stepped into the leadership vacuum (created by Speaker Gingrich's resignation) and blocked a censure alternative. Censure was the option favored by most Americans and many in Congress. Orchestrating events from behind the scenes, DeLay succeeded in crushing all attempts to consider censure the moment they arose. As a result, moderate Congressmen on both sides had no middle ground to vote their consciences.

DeLay realized that the Senate would not convict. His real mission was to drive Clinton from office: first impeach, and then force him to resign. He ordered his staff to "dedicate yourselves to it or leave" and "to work day and night." He took this step in mid-August 1998, a month **before** Starr submitted his findings to Congress. [42]

Throughout, DeLay left nothing to chance. For example, he set up a special "evidence room" where he and his deputies would send undecided House members. This room included allegations which not even Starr saw fit to publish, much of them uncorroborated and undocumented. [43] Using his powerful Whip position, DeLay applied intense pressure on House members who were wavering or on the fence by:

- Threatening loss chairmanships.
- Threatening to arrange strong challenges in their next Congressional races.
- Threatening to turn fund raisers and party officials against them.
- Threatening to expose them to their constituents if they visited the "evidence room" and still cleared Clinton. [44]

A member of DeLay's staff was quoted as telling one Republican Congressman who opposed impeachment that "...the next two years would be the longest of his life." Later, Bob Woodward would report that Chairman Hyde was willing to entertain censure had his leadership been willing. [45]

Public Up in Arms—Petitions Congress

Much of the public was alarmed by what was going on in Congress, but was unable to stop it. As just one example: a young couple in California set up an organization on the Internet called *Censure and MoveOn* [46] About forty *MoveOn* volunteers went to Washington, at their own expense, to deliver more than 300,000 anti-impeachment petitions to House members from their constituents.

In addition, *MoveOn* delivered, in the presence of the media, a full set of the petitions to the House Speaker's office. These petitions urged the House to censure the President and move on with the country's business. They were signed by Democrats, Republicans, and Independents alike. [47]

MoveOn volunteers also made 250,000 phone calls and sent a million e-mails to Congress. Millions of other people also expressed opposition and eventually, lines of communication to Washington broke down. [48]

Right-Wing Leaders Defy Founding Fathers/U.S. Constitution

Former President Ford said an impeachable offense "is whatever a majority of the House of Representatives considers it to be at a given moment in history." As the history of impeachment shows he surely must have been jesting.[49]

The impeachment of a president is a modern day, civilized alternative to assassination of a king. To avoid Britain's partisan misuse of impeachment and because our constitutional framers distrusted legislatures, they limited its use to *grave breaches* of official duties, specifically *treason and bribery*.

When our framers added *"other high crimes and misdemeanors,"* the term *"other"* obviously meant something on a par with treason and bribery. The term *"high misdemeanors"* actually refers to serious offenses against the state as in 18th century England, not minor or trivial offenses as we interpret misdemeanors today. As one framer said, we are talking about *"great and dangerous offenses."*[50]

In 1998, 400 historians and 430 law professors warned the House against impeachment. The law professors said members of Congress would violate their constitutional responsibilities if they sought to remove the President for reasons that fell short of constitutional standards. Many scholars agreed with George Mason's statement that impeachment must be for a great crime or an attempt to subvert the Constitution.

Another founding father, James Madison, opposed a low standard because it would create a weak presidency serving at the pleasure of Congress. The framers of our Constitution obviously wanted the highest possible bar for removal of a president.[51]

Alexander Hamilton warned "the greatest danger [is] that the decision [to impeach] will be regulated more by the comparative strength of the parties, than by the real demonstrations of innocence or guilt."[52] As a House member later confirmed, the strength of the parties did, in fact, regulate the outcome.

"When radical Republicans hijacked the Constitution and misused impeachment for partisan purposes, I worked on the House Judiciary Committee in an effort to stop them. We lost all the votes along party lines....While we couldn't dissuade Republicans in the House

of Representatives, the overwhelming voice of Americans helped the
United States Senate to end this madness."[53]

Representative Zoe Lofgren

Common sense tells us that our founding fathers put impeachment in the Constitution to deal with such things as serious breaches of official duties and great crimes against society. If impeachment, instead, concerned covering up a personal indiscretion, some of our founding fathers (like Thomas Jefferson) may have been vulnerable, as would some of our fine national leaders of the recent times (Presidents Roosevelt, Eisenhower and Kennedy).

The impeachment remedy was intended to preserve constitutional government by removing from office an official who subverts the office, not someone who covers up a private and personal matter.[54]

The general public had expressed its displeasure with what was going on in the House of Representatives by voting a major Republican setback and by voicing overwhelming objections. The public knew this was a private offense, not a public one against the state.

They also knew that there had to be a higher standard for removing a twice-elected president. The people who elected and reelected Clinton saw him as "a flawed but highly capable and essentially decent man." No evidence has ever emerged to connect Clinton's personal life with his performance as President.[55]

Conclusions and Remedies

The right-wing conspiracy against the President of the United States followed by misuse of our judicial system to plot his downfall was an attempt to undo an election by the American people. The Paula Jones case should have been stopped by the Supreme Court on constitutional grounds. A disruptive civil suit should never have been allowed to interfere with the President's official duties and his fulltime responsibilities to the American people.

Kenneth Starr had no authority to invade the President's private life. Even though misled by Starr, the Attorney General was in a position to stop his intrusion had she followed her own statutory review requirements and judicial ethics on conflicts of interest.

Both Ken Starr and Chairman Hyde have since publicly confessed regret. In December 2004, Starr acknowledged that Whitewater and Lewinsky were "separate" matters and that he should *not* have led the Lewinsky one. Starr's excesses eventually led to the demise of the law that created him. Asked whether he would do the impeachment again, Judiciary Chairman Hyde said, "I'm not sure. I might not."[56]

After Starr became a puppet of right-wing House leaders and violated his own statute to advocate impeachment, Minority Whip Tom DeLay's abuse of power forced it through the House. The impeachment had nothing to do with presidential performance and disregarded our Constitution.

The House impeachment action and the Senate trial that followed distracted Congress from fulfilling its responsibility to deal with the gathering threat of international terrorism. As the 9/11 Commission subsequently reported, "Congress took too little action to address the emerging terrorism threat." (It) gave little guidance to agencies, did not reform them to meet the threat, and did not perform robust oversight."

The only sure way to prevent such abuses in the future is to have an informed public and hold those responsible personally accountable. Unless the right wing is held accountable for trying to nullify two of the Clinton presidential elections, our system of government will continue to be subjected to win-at-any-cost methods and could suffer grave consequences – as it eventually did (See chapters two through six).

House leaders responsible for abuses of power and constitutional violations are no longer in Congress. Three resigned in disgrace because of personal indiscretions or violations of office (Gingrich, Livingston and DeLay) and the fourth retired (Hyde). Three of these four gentlemen had or were having extra-marital affairs.

The House Ethics committee later admonished Tom DeLay for attempted bribery to get a House member's vote and for soliciting contributions for legislative favors. Several of his associates have been indicted for laundering illegal contributions and DeLay himself was subjected to criminal investigation for a number of years before being convicted of money laundering in 2010. He was sentenced to three years in prison. That case is under appeal.[57]

DeLay was also involved in violations of House voting rules, unfair redrawing of House districts to favor Republicans and misuse of Homeland Security resources to settle a dispute over drawing a new House district in Texas.[58]

The most precious thing we have in our democracy is the right to choose our local and national leaders, including the President of the United States. Subversive politics challenged that right, disrupted our nation and weakened our presidency and national security on the gathering threat of terrorism. To prevent recurrence, Congress should:

- Set a higher bar and reasonable time limits for investigations of a president. This would mean not clouding a presidency with politically-motivated investigations and allowing them to drag on without conclusions throughout his term in office.

- Establish constitutional standards for initiating impeachment proceedings of a president in accordance with the intent of our founders and the Constitution. The purpose is to prevent further use of impeachment as a political tool to drive a president from office.

Legacy of a President the Right Wing Wanted to Remove from Office

- Made the Democratic Party competitive again by moving it toward the center.
- Brought the country into fiscal responsibility and, for the first time in decades, started paying down the national debt.
- Pushed the United States headlong into the global economy.
- Presided over the most successful economy in history, while at the same time strengthening controls over damages to our environment.
- Became a highly respected world leader, improving relations with other countries and acting as a global peacekeeper.

- Raised the stature of women and minorities generally, got millions off welfare and, for the first time in history, chose a cabinet that reflected a true cross-section of the American society.
- Made a heroic attempt to resolve the Palestinian/Israel conflict.
- Demonstrated an amazing grasp of the issues and a wonderful ability to communicate them to the American people.
- Is now a world statesman and problem solver for the most unfortunate and distressed caused by circumstances beyond their control.

Lessons Learned From the Impeachment

1. When a woman remains quiet for several years and then suddenly sues the President of the United States for sexual harassment, it's not about harassment – it's about dirty politics.
2. When a Supreme Court blunders in matters of partisan politics, our country ought to find a better way of choosing justices and a way to remove them when they violate the public's right to a fulltime president. The Court further contributed to the right-wing conspiracy by deciding that the Independent Council function was constitutional, although it was actually a fourth branch of government with an unlimited budget. (See chapter seven for other illegitimate Supreme Court decisions.)
3. When an Independent Counsel sets aside several investigations to work on a cover-up of a private, consensual matter, it is because his other investigations are coming up empty and his political supporters are terribly unhappy with him.
4. When media reporters lick the Independent Counsel's boots and do not challenge the underlying political conspiracy, they are being controlled with leaked information and the Independent Counsel is the "leaker"
5. When the same Independent Counsel contravenes his statue and becomes an advocate for impeachment, it should have been clear to everyone that his intentions were always to bring down the President.
6. When a House Judiciary Chairman promises the American people to establish impeachment standards and hold bipartisan hearings and

delivers neither, something is going on behind the scenes in Congress and the media and the American people ought to seriously worry about it. The media did not, but the American people did.

7. When impeachment hearings are inordinately rushed with no direct witnesses called, the question must be asked whether a political conspiracy is at work.

8. When power-obsessed House leaders are proceeding with impeachment of a President of the opposite party, in disregard of the Constitution, their actions can damage the country in many unforeseen ways, as they eventually did (See chapters two through six).

———

" … The true crime: the attempted assassination of the President's character, a crushing of his person, an evisceration of his inner life so that the details were set out to be picked over on television … by the Sunday sorts who mistakenly thought the scandal was about what Mr. Clinton had done and not what was being done to him."

Richard Cohen, Washington Post, Feb. 10, 1999

ENDNOTES

1. Blinded By the Right: The Conscience of an Ex-Conservative, David Brock, Crown Publishers, 2002, pp. 79-81.
2. The Hunting Of The President: The Ten-Year Campaign to Destroy Bill and Hillary Clinton, Joe Conason and Gene Lyons, St. Martin's Press, 2000, pp. 104-107, 259.
3. Ibid, pp. 139-153.
4. Ibid, p. 111.
5. Ibid, p. 174.
6. A Vast Conspiracy, Jeffrey Toobin, Touchstone, 2000, pp. 81-82.
7. The Clinton Wars, Sidney Blumenthal, Farrar, Strauss and Giroux, 2003, pp. 537-538.
8. Blinded By the Right, David Brock, p. 143.
9. "Anti-Clinton Lawyers Kept Jones' Case Alive," Don Van Natta and Jill Abramson, *New York Times*, January 24, 1999.
10. Blinded By the Right, David Brock, pp. 179-183.
11. "Anti-Clinton Lawyers Kept Jones' Case Alive," Don Van Natta and Jill Abramson, *New York Times*, January 24, 1999.
12. Blinded By the Right, David Brock, pp. 184-185.
13. Ibid, pp. 190-191.
14. "Rulebook? What Rulebook?" Alan Ehrenhalt, *New York Times*.
15. Blinded By the Right, David Brock, p. 188.
16. A Vast Conspiracy, Jeffrey Toobin, p. 93.

17. Blinded By the Right, David Brock, p. 310.
18. The Clinton Wars, Sidney Blumenthal. p.791.
19. A Vast Conspiracy, Jeffrey Toobin, pp. 188-189.
20. Ibid, p. 94.
21. Blinded By the Right, David Brock, p. 301.
22. The Hunting Of The President, Conason and Lyons, p. 259.
23. "With its cloudy decisions, Supreme Court ignores reality," David Broder, Washington Post, March 31, 1998.
24. The Hunting Of The President, Conason and Lyons, pp. 259-264.
25. "Pressgate," Steven Brill, Brill's Content, p. 127.
26. "Reno Has Bungled the Lewinsky Case," Thomas Oliphant, Boston Globe, June 30, 1998.
27. "Pressgate," Steven Brill, Brill's Content, p. 127.
28. Ibid, p. 128.
29. The Hunting Of The President, Conason and Lyons, pp. 356-357.
30. Ibid, p. 127.
31. Ibid, pp. 356-357; Blinded By the Right, David Brock, p. 317.
32. Blinded By the Right, David Brock, p. 317.
33. A Vast Conspiracy, Jeffrey Toobin, p. 202.
34. "Reno Has Bungled the Lewinsky Case," Thomas Oliphant, Boston Globe, June 30, 1998.
35. Shadow: Five Presidents and the Legacy of Watergate, Bob Woodard, Simon and Schuster, 1999, p. 516.
36. "Sam Dash's November 20, 1998 letter to Kenneth Starr," Blumenthal, The Clinton Wars, pp. 518-519.
37. "U.S. Never Had Firm Grasp on Terrorism," Judith Miller, Jeff Gerth and Don Van Natta, New York Times.
38. The Clinton Wars, Sidney Blumenthal, pp. 484, 539, 587-588.
39. E-mail from Zoe Lofgren, Member of Congress, to MoveOn, February 12, 1999.
40. The Breach: Inside the Impeachment and Trial of William Jefferson Clinton, Peter Baker, Simon and Schuster, 2000, p. 204.
41. Ibid, p. 16.
42. Ibid, pp. 252, 263.
43. Ibid, pp. 43-44.

44. Ibid, pp. 16, 138, 231-232.

45. The Clinton Wars, Sidney Blumenthal pp. 537-539.

46. Shadow: Five Presidents and the Legacy of Watergate, pp. 484-489.

47. "Grass-Roots Organizing Effort Gets a Big Boost from Internet," Melissa Healy, *Los Angeles Times*, January 13, 1999.

48. Censure and MoveOn press release, December 15, 1998.

49. Original MoveOn Website.

50. A Vast Conspiracy, Jeffrey Toobin, p. 334.

51. Ibid, p. 333.

52. Clinton Wars, David Blumenthal, pp. 490-504.

53. "Criminal? Possibly, Impeachable? No," Herman Schwartz, *Los Angeles Times.*

54. Letter from Zoe Lofgren to MoveOn, February 10, 1999.

55. "Criminal? Possibly, Impeachable? No," *Los Angeles Times.*

56. The Hunting Of The President, Conason and Lyons, pp. 370-371.

57. "Kenneth Starr says he shouldn't have been involved in the Lewinsky case," *Associated Press*, December 2, 2004; "Rep. Hyde reflects on 30 years of office," Andy Shaw, *ABC 7, Chicago.com*, April 22, 2005.

58. "DeLay convicted of money-laundering charges in campaign finance scheme," Robert Barnes and Jeffrey Smith, *Washington Post,* Nov. 25, 2010.

59. "DeLay to Be Subject of Ethics Complaint," Charles Babington, *Washington Post*, June 15, 2004. The following are other articles on DeLay's ethics and the legality of his practices:

"GOP Comes Around to Majority View, Andrea Stone and William M. Welch," *USA Today*, June 17, 2004.

"Tom DeLay's Amoral Code," Katrina vanden Heuvel, *The Nation*, June 23, 2005.

"Ethics committee awaits DeLay's response," Rachna Sheth, *The Daily Texan*, July 2, 2004.

"DeLay's Corporate Fundraising Investigated," Jeffrey Smith, *Washington Post*, July 12, 2005.

"Curbing GOP's iron rule in Congress," Marty Meehan, *boston.com*, July 16, 2004.

"House rejects outside probe of majority leader," *Associated Press*, October 9, 2004.

"GOP should ask DeLay to quit leadership post," Editorial Board, *statesman.com*, October 10, 2004.

"Breaking News...DeLay Gets Served," Jesselee, *The Stateholder*, October 21, 2004.

"House Ethics Panel in Gridlock," Mike Allen, *Washington Post*, March 11, 2005.

"DeLay And Company," Karen Tumulty, *Times Online Edition*, March 14, 2005.

"Defiant DeLay Dirty Dealings," *The Center for American Progress/ Progress Report*, March 16, 2005.

Book Sources

Peter Baker, The Breach: Inside the Impeachment and Trial of William Jefferson Clinton, Simon and Schuster, 2000.

Sidney Blumenthal, The Clinton Wars, Farrar, Strauss and Giroux, 2003.

David Brock, Blinded By the Right: The Conscience of an Ex-Conservative, Crown Publishers, 2002.

Joe Conason and Gene Lyons, The Hunting Of The President: The Ten-Year Campaign to Destroy Bill and Hillary Clinton, St. Martin's Press, 2000.

Jeffery Toobin, A Vast Conspiracy, Touchstone, 2000.

Bob Woodward, Shadow: Five Presidents and the Legacy of Watergate, Simon and Schuster, 1999.

Chapter Two

———•◦•———

NOW IN CHARGE, RIGHT-WING ADMINISTRATION DOES NOT RESPOND TO EXTRAORDINARY WARNINGS OF IMPENDING 9/11 ATTACKS

F aced with a declaration of war, a history of previous attacks and unprecedented warnings of new ones, the right-wing administration took no action to defend the nation or inform the public of the impending danger. It had knowledge that:

- The former President, the CIA and top experts considered the al-Qaeda network the gravest and most immediate threat to the United States.
- Three Heads of State and other friendly countries were warning us of a major catastrophe about to befall our nation.
- These warnings disclosed Al-Qaeda's intent to seize our aircraft and use them as weapons and that its members were here in the U.S. planning the attacks and learning to fly.

From the outset, then President George W. Bush, Vice-President Richard Cheney, and their national security team did not give the al-Qaeda threat the attention it deserved. As the threat grew and became more menacing, they made no attempt to prevent the attacks, or to protect commercial aviation, or to inform the public of the danger.

For a look at how the most advanced threat in decades had developed into a clear and present danger, we begin with its gradual emergence during the 90's.

Terrorism Under the Clinton Administration

The first attack on the New York World Trade Center occurred in late 1993. It killed six individuals and injured hundreds more. Those directly responsible were captured and sent to prison.[1]

In 1996, terrorists bombed a U. S. military complex in Saudi Arabia, killing nineteen American servicemen. In the same year, Osama Bin Laden declared a holy war against Americans for occupying Saudi Arabia.[2] In late 1998, this threat to the United States took on new meaning when Bin Laden announced a declaration of war and bombed two of our embassies, killing 224 people and injuring about 5,000.

In response, President Clinton became the first President to coordinate counterterrorism directly from the White House and have the chief coordinator report directly to him. The President responded to the attacks by:

- More than doubling anti-terrorism budgets.
- Launching cruise missiles at al-Qaeda training camps.
- Trying diplomatically to have Bin Laden expelled from Afghanistan.
- Authorizing a CIA death warrant – covert authority to capture or kill Bin Laden and his chief lieutenants.
- Developing the improved Predator, an unmanned aircraft with video capable of spying on al-Qaeda training camps and recognizing Bin Laden (now called "drones").
- Arming the Predator with a hellfire missile so that Bin Laden could be found and killed in real time.[3]
- Beginning a global crackdown on terrorist funding involving some thirty industrial nations.

One cruise missile hit an al-Qaeda training camp, but Bin Laden had already departed; another struck the wrong target due to bad intelligence. Some subsequent Clinton efforts to take out Bin Laden were aborted.

Either the CIA Director pulled the plug or the White House national security team rejected the plans on the grounds that they were unworkable or based on dubious intelligence. Clinton insisted that he personally receive a pipeline of daily reports on al-Qaeda. His staff considered him obsessed on the subject.

At the turn of the century, Clinton exercised widespread precautions to prevent domestic attacks and made the public fully aware of potential dangers. The CIA and FBI worked frantically to uncover millennium plots. Several were disrupted and one attack involving the Los Angeles Airport was halted.[4]

Just before the 2000 presidential election, al-Qaeda struck again — this time the target was the U.S.S. Cole. The ship almost sank and we lost seventeen servicemen. The strike prompted the Clinton administration to prepare a bold plan of attack to rout al-Qaeda in Afghanistan. At the time of presidential transition, however, responsibility for U.S.S. Cole attack was still under FBI investigation.

Clinton decided he could not respond without proof of responsibility, especially since the CIA/military operation he contemplated would have to be conducted by the new administration. So the bold attack plan was passed on in special briefings with Vice-President Richard Cheney and National Security Advisor Condoleezza Rice. According to an unnamed senior Bush official, the Clinton plan contained all the steps taken soon after September 11, 2001.[5]

During transition, President Clinton and his team warned the incoming administration at the very highest levels that Bin Laden and al-Qaeda would be their greatest concern.

Terrorism Under the Bush Administration

In January 2001, at the outset of the new Bush administration, CIA Director George Tenet warned Congress in open testimony that "the threat from terrorism is real, it is immediate, and it is evolving." He said that Bin Laden and his global network remained the most immediate and serious threat to U.S interests and that Bin Laden had declared all U.S. citizens to be legitimate targets. He testified further that Bin Laden is capable of planning multiple attacks with little or no warning.

However, one of the first actions taken by White House was to downgrade the counter-terrorism unit. It no longer had access to the President and heads of agencies.[6] In late January 2001, the head of this counter-terrorism unit urgently requested a cabinet-level meeting on the al-Qaeda threat. He reported that there were al-Qaeda cells in the United States and that we would make a major error if we underestimated the threat. No meeting was held.[7]

Clinton's global crackdown on terrorist funding was abandoned by the new administration in response to a powerful banking lobby. Clinton's bold response to the U.S.S. Cole attack became a "victim of not invented here, turf wars and time spent on pet policies of top Bush officials."[8]

Reinforcing President Clinton's warnings to the new administration were two U.S. bipartisan commissions, one on national security and the other on terrorism. The two commissions reported that a major terrorist attack was inevitable and urged that our defenses be bolstered.

For example, the U.S. Commission on National Security for the 21st Century reported at the end of January 2001 that the United States was vulnerable to a catastrophic terrorist attack and that many lives might be lost. In White House meetings, the Commission Chair urged the creation of a National Homeland Security Agency. Congress was seriously interested and wanted to hold hearings on the subject.

The President rejected the new agency and cut a deal with Congress – lawmakers would drop the hearings on terrorism and the new agency, and the President would turn over to the Vice President a "national effort" to respond to domestic attacks. That project never really got off the ground and could not have met its October 2001deadline.[9]

Paul Bremer headed the bipartisan commission on terrorism which had completed its work several months earlier. In a speech in February 2001, he concluded that the Bush administration was:

> "...paying no attention to the problem of terrorism ... what they will do is stagger along until there's a major incident and then suddenly say, 'Oh my God, shouldn't we be organized to deal with this?' ... They've been given a window of opportunity ... and they're not taking advantage of it." [10]

Also in February 2001, Vice-President Cheney received a briefing that Bin Laden's al-Qaeda network was indeed responsible for the U.S.S. Cole attack. Barton Gellman's Pulitzer Prize winning book (*Angler – The Cheney Vice-Presidency*) notes that during the spring the Vice-President received at least five recommendations in writing for a military response to the U.S.S. Cole. No action was taken.[11]

During the presidential campaign, Bush had said "there must be a consequence" for the U.S.S. Cole. Now in charge, he did not respond to the attack or resume the CIA death warrant against Bin Laden. During the campaign, Cheney had said, "Any would-be terrorist needs to know that if you're going to attack, you'll be hit very hard and very quick." He went on to say: "It's not time for diplomacy and debate. It's time for action." Given the opportunity to do both, he did neither.[12]

The remotely controlled unmanned Predator (called "Operation Afghan Eyes") was the best possible source of intelligence on what was going on in Bin Laden's terrorist camps. However, the program got bogged down because of Department of Defense/Central Intelligence Agency bureaucratic infighting over who would control the program, pay for it and have authority to shoot the new hellfire missile. Vice-President Cheney, who had the lead role in the White House, and Cabinet-rank advisors were unable to resolve the issue. The Predator was sitting idle on September 11th.

During the spring of 2001, frantic warnings of impending al-Qaeda attacks began to surface from reliable sources around the world. By the summer, they had reached a crescendo.

Heads of State and Our Allies Repeatedly Warn of Impending Attacks

Portions of Bin Laden's 9/11 plans had gradually seeped out to intelligence agencies around the world. Our allies, in turn, relayed this information to us. Of the many allies reporting, some just gave frantic warnings while others identified (1) a time frame, (2) the presence of al-Qaeda members in our country and (3) the actual means of attack.

The warnings below are fully documented in the book, The Terror Timeline: Year By Year, Day By Day, Minute By Minute, A Comprehensive

Chronicle of the Road to 9/11 and America's Response. They are omitted from the 9/11 Commission report. [14]

- March 2001 – Based on wiretaps, Italy warned the U.S. of a "very, very secret" plan and the forging of documents for al-Qaeda agents to be sent to the United States. One of the callers sounded like a previous one who had described a massive strike involving aircraft.

- April – An Afghanistan source reported an al-Qaeda plot to attack the U.S. in suicide missions involving airplanes. The source said Al-Qaeda agents were already in place inside the U.S. and were being trained as pilots.

- May – Key al-Qaeda operatives reported leaving Afghanistan to go to the U.S., Canada and Great Britain – while others were preparing for martyrdom.

- May-July – The National Security Agency picked up thirty-three (classified) communications about impending attacks.

- June – Germany warned the CIA of terrorist plans to hijack commercial aircraft and use them as missiles against U.S. and Israel targets.

- June - Bin Laden said in a TV interview "coming weeks will hold important surprises that will target American and Israeli interests."

- July – Egypt warned that twenty al-Qaeda members had slipped into the U.S. Four of them were training to fly. Egypt had informants inside al-Qaeda.

- July – Due to fear of severe U.S. retaliation, the Afghanistan Foreign Minister warned local consul and U.N. officials of huge attacks on targets inside U.S. that would kill thousands.

- July – Argentina relayed a warning to us from reliable sources of an attack of major proportions against the United States.

- July and **again** in August – England warned us of "a very serious threat" involving multiple airplane hijackings and that al-Qaeda was in the final stages of preparing the attack. British spy agencies and Prime Minister Blair participated. Warnings were said to have reached President Bush.

- Late summer – Jordan warned twice that aircraft would be used in a major attack inside the U.S., code named "The Big Wedding." The warnings were deemed so important that one message was sent to the U.S. through the Jordanian King's men and the second to the U.S. through Germany. Following 9/11, the Bush administration reportedly had Jordan retract the warnings. "The Big Wedding" was al-Qaeda's code for 9/11.

- August – Israel warned that a "major assault on the U.S. was imminent" and gave us a terrorist list of persons residing in U.S. Four actual hijackers were on the list.

- August – Morocco warned that Bin Laden planned a large scale operation in summer or fall and he was very disappointed that the 1993 World Trade Center attack had failed. Information came from a source who had penetrated al-Qaeda deeply enough to be close to Bin Laden.

- August – Russia's Vladimir Putin instructed his intelligence people to warn President Bush "in strongest possible terms" that pilots were in training for suicide missions on U.S. targets. Following 9/11, the Russian head of intelligence said "we had clearly warned them on several occasions."

- August – France echoed the earlier Israel warning.

- August — Egypt warned us that al-Qaeda was in the advanced stages of planning significant attack on the U.S. Following 9/11, President Mubarak confirmed that this warning was sent.[15]

- August — A former CIA agent passed along information from a Persian Gulf informant of a "spectacular terrorist operation" that would occur shortly.

A 2002 House/Senate joint inquiry into pre-9/11 intelligence found similar warnings on use of aircraft as weapons stretching through the summer of 2001.[16] The 9/11 Commission report omitted these House/Senate findings.

Urgency of Threat Couldn't "Get Any Worse"

Counter-terrorism officials thought the warnings were "the most urgent in decades." Intelligence reporting referred to the upcoming attacks as "occurring on a calamitous level ... causing the world to be in turmoil and that they would consist of multiple — but not necessarily simultaneous — attacks." Secretary of State Colin Powell referred to the warnings as an impending Hiroshima on U.S. soil.[17]

In late June, CIA Director Tenet sent an intelligence summary to the White House and met personally with National Security Advisor Condi Rice. Among other things, he reported: "It is highly likely that a significant al-Qaeda attack will occur within several weeks." Tenet added: "Most of the al-Qaeda network is anticipating an attack..." Based on a review of all source reporting over the last five months, he said:

"We believe that (bin Laden) will launch a significant attack against U.S. and/or Israeli interests in the coming weeks. The attack will be spectacular and designed to inflict mass casualties ... Attack preparations have been made. Attack will occur with little or no warning"... "This is going to be a big one."[18]

A June 30th CIA briefing to top administration officials said Bin Laden operatives expected the attack would have dramatic consequences of catastrophic proportions.[19]

By July, according to the CIA Director, the "system was blinking red" and later in the month he said the warnings could not "get any worse."[20] Based on communications intercepts and other top-secret intelligence, Tenet and his Counterterrorism Chief had developed a compelling case that al-Qaeda would soon attack the United States. As confided to Bob Woodward (in his book *State of Denial*), the CIA Director took the unusual step of making a hurried and unscheduled visit to the White House to brief the President's national security team.[21]

During the meeting, Tenet urged a military attack to remove al-Qaeda from its sanctuary in Afghanistan and asked for covert authority for his organization to proceed against Bin Laden and his lieutenants. This was his second request for the same covert authority that Clinton had previously given him. The CIA Director believed the time to act was **at that very moment** – military and covert – to thwart Bin Laden.

This was the starkest warning given the White House to date. The CIA Director left the meeting "feeling frustrated." because "no immediate action meant great risk."[22] The 9/11 Commission omitted this crucial White House meeting from its report.

Later in August, the CIA head of counterterrorism made a public speech on the subject, saying "we are going to be attacked soon … many Americans are going to die."[23] Two counterterrorism officials were so concerned that they considered resigning to go public. According to *Time Magazine's* "Special Report on 9/11," a frustrated high ranking FBI official in New York did resign and became security chief of the World Trade Center. He did not survive the attack.[24]

In August, the CIA Director made a special trip to Crawford Texas to brief the President on the FBI arrest of the man who would have been the 20th hijacker. He was arrested with a lot of unexplained cash and was hurriedly learning how to take off and land a Boeing 747.[25] As will be discussed later, the President and CIA Director declined to acknowledge that this briefing took place, but the meeting has since been confirmed.

The White House Does Not Respond

CIA Director Tenet briefed the President, Vice-President, and National Security Advisor regularly on the al-Qaeda threat, and he briefed other top officials (like Defense Secretary Donald Rumsfeld, Secretary of State Powell and Attorney General George Ashcroft) as needed.

CIA Director Tenet felt that the best solution was to go on the offense and dislodge al-Qaeda from its sanctuary in Afghanistan, or else Bin Laden would continue to operate with impunity and recruit and train more Islamic extremists. It would just be a matter of time before he would do more damage to the United States. Tenet proposed a joint operation – CIA covert authorities plus teams of military Special Forces to attack al Qaeda training camps and take out Bin Laden.[26]

White House **Chief Counterterrorism Coordinator Richard Clarke** tried at various times to get the attention of top decision makers and conducted interagency meetings on defensive security alerts. He had conceived the Clinton attack plan that was passed on to top Bush officials, including National Security Advisor Rice. That plan was consistent with CIA Director Tenet's approach, but was not acted upon until immediately after the 9/11 attacks. It was creative and amazingly simple:

> • *Support the ongoing Afghan resistance (Northern Alliance) against the Taliban government so that al-Qaeda training graduates would have to stay in Afghanistan to fight and die for the Taliban. (Note: Al-Qaeda feared the Northern Alliance – two associates, disguised as journalists, murdered the Northern Alliance leader just two days before the 9/11 attacks.)*

> • *Use the unmanned Predator to locate al-Qaeda training camps, conduct air strikes and then use U.S. Special Forces to destroy the training camps and kill or capture Bin Laden.*[27]

By late June, Clarke had sent two letters to National Security Advisor Rice – one describing several reports of al-Qaeda personnel talking about a pending attack and the other saying that al-Qaeda's activity had reached a "crescendo." Desperate to get top level attention, he said: "When these attacks occur ... we will wonder what more we could have done to stop them" and "imagine a future day when hundreds of Americans lay dead."[28]

According to Acting FBI Director Tom Pickard, **Attorney General John Ashcroft** appeared disinterested and denied a request for $50 million in terrorist funding. His priorities for the FBI and his goals for the Justice Department omitted counterterrorism. According to Pickard, Ashcroft asked not to be briefed on this subject again. However, after July, Ashcroft began flying expensive charters rather than commercial aircraft because of an "official threat assessment."[29]

During the months leading up to the 9/11 attacks, **Defense Secretary Rumsfeld** was A.W.O.L. The Defense Secretary still had not filled his Department's key position on counterterrorism. According to the 9/11 Commission report, he did not asked the Joint Chiefs to furnish military options for the al-Qaeda threat. At 9/11, there still was no military mission for the al-Qaeda network, although it was the most dangerous enemy the U.S. faced at the time.[30] Congress tried to divert $600 million from Rumsfeld's missile shield program to counterterrorism, but he stopped it by threatening a presidential veto.[31]

In a meeting with other agencies, Rumsfeld's deputy said: "I just don't understand why we are beginning by talking about this one man, Bin Laden ... Who cares about a little terrorist in Afghanistan?" Rumsfeld believed the al-Qaeda warnings were a grand deception. He later gave the 9/11 Commission a different story, however, saying he had given his "principle attention to other challenges."[32]

Vice-President Cheney and National Security Advisor Rice were at the center of the storm, but left few fingerprints. They were the President's chief advisors and attended many of the presidential daily briefings and special terrorist briefings.

Rice determined the agenda for National Security meetings, which the President and other top key members attended. She also had responsibility for interagency coordination on national security matters. During transition and the months leading up to 9/11, she received special briefings and other information on the severity of the al-Qaeda threat.

She worked near the Oval Office and her main job was to focus on problems of major concern to the President. Terrorism apparently was not one of them. On the day of the 9/11 attacks, she was supposed to give a speech on the ***"threats of today."*** Her speech promoted a missile shield defense against rogue states and contained no reference to the numerous warnings of upcoming al-Qaeda attacks. She, of course, never gave that speech.[33]

There were opportunities for Rice to pull together members of the National Security Council, lay out the alarming evidence and ask members to present their views front and center to the President. Outside experts, such as former Presidents and Secretaries of State, could have been called in for advice on what was essentially a war-time situation. The ideal time would have been just after the CIA Director's emergency visit to the White House pleading for military action "at this very moment".

The administration, and in particular National Security Advisor Rice, claimed no one had ever considered that terrorists might use airplanes as weapons. As previously shown, there were specific warnings of aircraft hijacking and their use as weapons.

In his new book, former Defense Secretary Rumsfeld acknowledges that the President presided "over a national security process that was marked with incoherent decision-making and policy drift."[34] David Ignatius, of the *Washington Post*, put it another way:

> "...nothing would have prevented the national security advisor from mobilizing anti-terrorism policy against al-Qaeda in the months before 9/11. That's what makes this story a tragedy – that existing institutions of government might have averted the disaster, if they had taken action".[35]

Vice-President Dick Cheney had the lead role in the White House on both terrorism and intelligence and was told repeatedly in CIA briefings that we are going to be hit again. As noted in Gellman's book on the Vice-Presidency, Cheney described the al-Qaeda warnings as a "noise in the system," saying he was not especially alarmed.[36] Yet, one has to wonder: How could dangerous warnings from differing and highly credible sources, all a part of a similar pattern, be considered a "noise in the system?"

Earlier in the spring, Cheney had helped derail congressional hearings on terrorism and the need for a new Homeland Security Agency by taking on the job himself of preparing a defense against domestic attacks. As noted earlier, his project never really got off the ground.

In his book on the Vice-Presidency, Gellman reports that President Bush agreed to chair a meeting of the National Security Council to review the Vice-President's plans for a defense against terrorist attacks. The President never did hold such a meeting. Gellman further discloses that a three-star general on the White House National Security staff (Donald Kerrick) found little interest in terrorism on the part of top officials, including the Vice-President.[37]

Cheney and Rumsfeld had worked together in a previous administration and had been close friends. If the Vice-President had taken an interest in the threat, the chances are that the Secretary of Defense would have too. The unwillingness of either Cheney or Rumsfeld to respond to the threat most likely paralyzed the administration's national security apparatus. Only the President could have made a difference.

President Bush never took control of the situation or put the nation in a crisis mode. Before 9/11, the President had received at least 40 CIA briefings on al-Qaeda and/or Bin Laden. In the now infamous briefing in Texas on August 6, 2001, the CIA told the President of al-Qaeda's determination "to attack within the United States."[38]

The CIA also told the President that al-Qaeda had operatives residing in the U.S. and that the FBI had found "patterns of suspicious activity consistent with preparations for hijacking." The CIA considered the August 6th briefing an opportunity to tell the President that the bin Laden threat was "both current and serious."[39] It was not the historical relic that National Security Advisor Rice alluded to when she testified before the 9/11 Commission.

Following the August 6th CIA briefing, the President remained on vacation for the balance of the month and did not:

- Call a National Security Council or cabinet meeting to coordinate a government response to the al-Qaeda threat.
- Ask the Joint Chiefs for military options.
- Grant the CIA Director his twice requested covert authority to kill or capture Bin Laden.

- Act on the obvious requirement to protect commercial aviation.
- Alert the American people to the danger.

Just before the 9/11 attacks, the National Security Council placed on the President's desk a strategy aimed at eliminating al-Qaeda in a three to five year time period. Such a long-term strategy could not possibly confront a threat that was imminent, one where the CIA Director had reported "The system was blinking red," The strategy deferred decisions on what to spend, which steps to implement and when.[40] The strategy obviously had no relevance to the immediate threat.

As the CIA Director had urged back in July, the time to act was now – that very moment. The CIA Director's private view, as confided to Bob Woodard of the *Washington Post*, was that "he had sounded the loudest warning he could – it hadn't been heeded." He thought the earlier White House meeting in July was a tremendous lost opportunity to prevent or disrupt the 9/11 attacks.[41]

The *Terror Timeline* book, which documents the many advance warnings from heads of state and friendly countries, has about 1400 entries based on thousands of sources. It concluded that:

> **"The public record reflects that the extreme focus on terrorism in place at the end of the Clinton administration dropped dramatically under the Bush administration. With few exceptions, little attention was paid to terrorism, even as the number of warnings reached unprecedented levels."[42]**

About a year after 9/11 and well before the 9/11 investigative Commission got underway, *Time Magazine* issued its cover story "Special Report on the Secret History of 9/11". Based on many sources in and out of Washington, this Report contained key information from fifteen important journalists from around the world. Time's cover story concluded that the major terrorist attack wasn't averted because of "a systemic collapse in the ability of Washington's national security apparatus to handle the terrorist threat."

The White House Cover-Up

After 9/11, the President's attitude on investigating this major attack on the U.S. homeland was just the opposite of what it logically should have been. Normally, a president would be anxious to work closely with an investigation to get at the heart of the problem and prevent future attacks. In this case, President Bush and Vice-President Cheney urged the Senate Majority Leader not to pursue an investigation and managed to block it for a year. [44]

However, the families of 9/11 victims and individual members of Congress persisted until legislation was eventually passed to create the 9/11 Commission. Pressured by the 9/11 family victims and by approaching midterm elections, the President changed his stance and signed the legislation.

The Bush administration then proceeded to stonewall the 9/11 Commission for much of its existence. It screened all Commission requests for information and intimidated agency officials by having monitors present at their Commission interviews. [45]

The White House stonewalling eventually caught the attention of the media. For example, The Wall Street Journal did an outstanding article on the subject. [46] Some Commissioners openly acknowledged lengthy delays, maddening restrictions and disputes over access to sensitive documents and witnesses. According to Commissioner Ben-Veniste, "a blow torch and pliers" were required to extract information. [47]

In the end, the Commission settled for less than full access to sensitive White House documents and, to get those, it had to threaten use of its subpoena power. Only a few selected Commission members were allowed access to sensitive documents, such as the presidential daily intelligence briefings. Their notes were subjected to White House review and security classification.

The Commission reviewers were limited as to what portions they could see and what portions could be shared with the full Commission. Objecting to these terms of access, one Commissioner immediately resigned. [48] Ultimately, the various delays required an extension of the Commission's reporting deadline to the rapidly approaching presidential election.

9/11 Commission Cover-Up of Incriminating Evidence

For the most part, members of the Commission were former politicians rather than experts. They were evenly divided politically – five Democrats and five Republicans. A presidential appointee (Republican) was put in charge as one of the President's conditions for signing the legislation. The members were all distinguished people with fine reputations.

The Commission's statutory requirements included (1) a full and complete accounting of the circumstances surrounding the attacks, (2) an assessment of U.S. preparedness for the attacks and (3) findings and conclusions for corrective action.[49]

The Commission hired a Staff Director (Philip Zelikow) who had previously co-authored a book with National Security Advisor Condi Rice. The two of them had also worked together on Bush's transition team. And, when Rice later became Secretary of State, he became her State Department Counselor.[50]

A book authored by 9/11 Commissioner Ben-Veniste, states that Zelikow had "blind spots" toward the administration and was too dominant a personality and too close to Condi Rice and the White House to be placed in charge of the investigative staff.[51] The Commission's choice of him as Staff Director presented a conflict of interest and was most unwise.

The President's one-year delay in approving this investigation moved the timing of the Commission's report to the presidential election year, not a good time for a politically-divided group with deeply-held party loyalty to reveal its assessment of White House preparedness for the attacks.

As the Commission neared its reporting deadline, partisan warfare broke out at public hearings among individual commissioners. The subject was White House responsibility. To help defend the administration, at least one Republican member had a direct pipeline to the White House.

The Commission's report highlighted individual failures in the bureaucracy, but reached no conclusions on top level responsibility. It contained findings on and recommendations for the intelligence community, FBI, immigration, Congress, etc, – but, none on the White House, its national security apparatus or presidential leadership.

The partisan split and the approaching presidential election made it difficult for the Commissioners to gain a consensus on White House responsibility. Eventually, the Commission decided to report only facts and leave readers to draw their own conclusions. [52] There were several problems with this decision.

- The Commission's report omitted crucially important facts and so, how could the public reach the proper conclusions?
- The Commission decision not to assess White House responsibility was kept secret from the public and members of Congress and violated its own statutory mandate to assess U.S. preparedness.
- The Commission told the public and Congress in its report that "The most important failure was one of imagination,"[53] whereas a number of heads of state and friendly countries had earlier notified the administration of the actual means of attack. Among the most serious omissions from the Commission report were:

    —The specific warnings from heads of state and foreign allies of the upcoming attacks and the anticipated use of hijacked aircraft as weapons.

    —The CIA Director's final desperate act in July pleading with the White House to make an immediate response to the al-Qaeda threat.

    —Any explanation for the President's failure to respond to top level expert advice from (a) the previous President, (b) the two U.S. national security commissions, (c) the CIA Director and (d) the White House Chief Counterterrorism Coordinator.

    —Any explanation for important information contradicting the Commission report, such as the Joint Senate/House earlier revelations of use of hijacked aircraft as weapons and the Time Magazine special cover story about collapse of the administration's national security apparatus.[54]

The 9/11 Commission said senior (unnamed) officials across government share in the responsibility. It laid much of the blame on intelligence, FBI and immigration.[55]

However, any meaningful response by those departments to the threat was severely handicapped by the absence of leadership from the President and Vice-President. These two top officials, not the lower levels, had the benefit of numerous warnings of the impending attacks, frequent CIA briefings outlining the threat, and expert advice from multiple sources, such as the White House chief of counterterrorism and President Clinton.

The question never answered in the Commission report was what should any prudent president do when confronted with an al-Qaeda declaration of war, a history of earlier attacks, strong advice on the gravity of the threat, and specific and repeated warnings from credible sources of additional attacks underway?

Subsequent Challenges to 9/11 Commission Report

Based on interviews with 9/11 Commissioners and key staff members, Elizabeth Drew concluded in *The New York Review of Books* that "In an effort to achieve a unanimous, bipartisan report, the Commission decided not to assign individual blame and avoided overt criticism of the President himself." She reported further:

> *"They also knew that if they explicitly blamed Bush and his administration for failures to prevent the attacks, the energies of the White House and its political allies (including those in the press and television) would have been devoted to discrediting their work."*[56]

Commissioners have since begun to break ranks from their agreement to withhold conclusions on White House responsibility. Commissioner Ben-Veniste was the first to disclose on CNN the absence of conclusions on presidential responsibility in their report. In a new book, in 2009, he spoke more candidly:

> *"The summer of 2001 marked the most elevated threat level we had ever experienced, providing convincing evidence that a*

spectacular attack was about to occur", and after being told Bin Laden was determined to strike inside the United States, "the President had done absolutely nothing to follow up." [57]

Commissioner Bob Kerrey expressed his view in even blunter terms in an earlier 2006 film, entitled *9/11: Press for Truth* (still on the Internet):

"The promise I made to keep this out of the campaign is over. Mr. President, you knew they were in the United States. You were warned by the CIA. You knew in July they were in the United States. You were told again in August that it was a dire threat. Didn't do anything to harden our border security. Didn't do anything to harden airport security. Didn't do anything to engage local law enforcement ... and didn't warn the American people. What did you do? Nothing as far as we can see." [58]

In 2009, the White House Chief Counterterrorism Coordinator, Richard Clarke, reported in two newspaper articles that the highest levels of government were negligent. In the *Washington Post article*, he said the White House had ignored the 9/11 warnings and feared their disclosure would eliminate a second presidential term. [59] In the *New York Daily News article* Clarke was more direct and personal:

"The historical record is pretty clear by now that Bush did virtually nothing about the repeated warnings to him that those cataclysmic attacks were coming. Unfortunately, I can personally attest to that". [60]

Conclusions and Remedies

Faced with warnings of an impending catastrophe, the Bush right-wing administration did not act with the required sense of urgency, lead a response to the threat, prepare a proper civil defense, or share crucial information with the American people. The threat had reached a heightened state and the timing was imminent. There was specific advance information about the hijacking of commercial airplanes and the presence of al-Qaeda members in this country learning to fly. Their presence in U.S. commercial flying schools could have been investigated.

The threat was real, possible targets were known and the timing was imminent. The intelligence came from reliable foreign sources, including three heads of state: the King of Jordan, the Prime Minister of England and the President of Russia. Taken individually, the threat information was highly disturbing but, collectively, it was overpowering.

It is especially important to recognize that the United States at this very time was virtually in a state of war with Bin Laden and al-Qaeda. Offensive action was more than justified by Bin Laden's earlier declarations of war, his previous attacks on this country and the near-frenzy warnings of new ones predicting mass casualties. This did not happen and, to this day, we still don't know why.

As the CIA Director had said months before the attacks, it surely was just a matter of time before Bin Laden would strike again. The President should have called his National Security Council together, approved the CIA request for covert action against Bin Laden and asked the Joint Chiefs for military options. In addition, no response to the U.S.S. Cole attack showed U.S. weakness and was a horrible mistake. Bin Laden was emboldened to strike once more.

It's entirely possible that the disaster could have been avoided if the President had maintained the priority toward terrorism of the previous administration, retaliated against al-Qaeda for the U.S.S. Cole attack and responded to the extraordinary warnings during the spring and summer of 2001.

These warnings dictated two actions by the President – one *offensive* and the other *defensive*.

An *offensive* action that made a lot of sense was the CIA/Chief Counterterrorism proposal to use (1) CIA covert authority, (2) the Taliban's enemy (the Northern Alliance) and (3) elite U.S. military Special Forces to dispose of al-Qaeda's safe haven in Afghanistan and capture or kill Bin Laden. The highly sophisticated unmanned Predator could have searched out al-Qaeda training camps and Bin Laden's whereabouts.

The obvious **defensive** action was for the President to alert the public and agency heads to the imminent danger and take immediate steps to protect commercial aviation.

To help prevent the catastrophe, the people of the United States needed to be highly aware and observant as they were at the turn of the century during the Clinton administration. Public awareness may be our best defense against terrorism. Public awareness halted the Los Angeles Airport attack (2000), grounded the fourth 9/11 hijacked aircraft in Pennsylvania (2001), prevented a Christmas day commercial aircraft explosion (2009) and stopped a Times Square explosion (2010).

Sharing the threat information across government and with the general public would have stimulated a new level of energy, creativity, and cooperation within and among federal and local agencies. This surely would have surfaced information from intelligence agencies, the FBI and commercial flying schools. It would have encouraged sharing of information and permitted the public to assist in averting or disrupting the attacks. With a reenergized government and public participation, the country could have averted this horrible tragedy.

To illustrate, some people within government had good information, but did not know or appreciate its importance. Without knowledge of the advance warnings, these people were not able to clearly connect the dots. The outcome of the following two cases would surely have been different if the President had alerted the public to the threat and asked agency heads to give the matter their personal attention.

- **An FBI field agent analysis in July suggested a Bin Laden scheme to send students to U.S. aviation schools to prepare them for future terrorist attacks. His curiosity had been aroused by the inordinate number of Muslims in training at Arizona flight schools and his fear that they would use explosives to destroy a plane in flight. No one at FBI headquarters connected the dots and the field memo died. [61]**

- **A French Muslim (named Zacarias Moussaoui) was attending a flying school and stood out because with little knowledge of flying, he was interested in learning in a few days only how to take off and land**

a Boeing 747. The FBI field people took him into custody in August for a visa violation, but they actually wanted headquarters' approval to inspect his laptop computer and discover why he was in flying school with a large sum of unexplained cash. Again, no one at headquarters connected the dots and would not approve the computer inspection. The FBI field person protested this decision to headquarters, saying that the suspect might be planning to hijack a plane and crash it "into the World Trade Center". [62]

On August 23, two and a half weeks before 9/11, the FBI did finally brief CIA Director Tenet about Moussaoui learning to "take off and land" a Boeing 747. The briefing was titled, "Islamic Extremist Learns To Fly." A day later, the CIA Director reportedly went to Crawford, Texas to brief the President. The Director has declined to acknowledge this visit, but the Office of the Press Secretary report of Bush activities at Crawford confirms it. The President was briefed again by the CIA Director on August 31.[63] Mr. Moussaoui was found guilty as the 20th hijacker and is now in an American prison for life.

The only reasonable thing to have done at the time was to put the country in a crisis mode and take immediate action to protect the nation—especially commercial aircraft. The measures taken should have shown a government in action, anxious to protect its citizens and determined to make it difficult for these terrorist attacks to succeed. That's all we could have expected – but no less.

Why weren't the public and federal/local agency leaders given a heads-up on what was surely an imminent threat – as President Clinton had done at the turn of the century? We may never know for sure, but the most likely reasons are (1) the administration's obsession with its own agenda and (2) the fear that public knowledge of possible terror attacks on the U.S. homeland would sink an already sagging economy and endanger the president's reelection.

A troubled economy had cost the President's father his second term. Soon after the 9/11 attacks the President did call on the American people to "go shopping."

The Commission report chapter, "The System is Blinking Red," concluded that the number and severity of reported threats were unparalleled and that many officials knew something terrible was planned. The fundamental problem with the 9/11 Commission report is that there was no comparison of the President's response to the severity of this threat and with what any reasonable and prudent person would have done under similar circumstances.

To comply with its statutory mandate, the Commission had no alternative but to assess preparedness of the White House and its national security apparatus for the attacks. An approaching presidential election should not have interfered with the Commission's legal and moral obligation to do so.

The Commission had two options. The first was for the Chairman to hold regular face to face meetings with commission members to review the evidence, allow each side to present their views and work toward a sustainable position.

If there was no chance of getting consensus on what went wrong, the second option was to go ahead with a unified position on the remaining parts of the report and issue a minority report on White House responsibility. Commission minority reports are not that uncommon.

The official 9/11 Commission report assessed blame across government and, therefore, held no one accountable. After the report was released, the scapegoats came from lower ranks and middle management. The brunt of the responsibility fell on the intelligence agencies, FBI, and immigration. Unless the official record is corrected, we will lose an important lesson in leadership and accountability at the very highest levels of government.

Had the President prevented the 9/11 attacks, terrorism would no longer be the number one issue it is today. He did not and ironically, it helped him get reelected. He chose New York City (a Democratic citadel) to host the Republican Convention near Ground Zero. The slogan was "Stay Safe: Reelect Bush."

The reader may wonder why the CIA Director has not yet gone public in all these years. There is a long history of special CIA relationships with their presidents. If anyone of them ever spoke out critically, it would ruin future relationships with presidents and perhaps, the CIA forever.

REMEDIES

Reopening Official Record on 9/11 Accountability

Some 9/11 widows have strongly opposed the Commission's work on the grounds that it did not assign any accountability for individual failures that allowed 9/11 to happen. They do not agree with the Commission's "simplistic conclusion" that there was a "failure of imagination."[64] Congress should reopen the official record on 9/11 so that history of and accountability for 9/11 is complete. The public and future historians deserve better information and analysis than they now have.

Requiring Accountability at Highest Levels of Government

By omitting crucial information and allowing politics to interfere with accountability, the 9/11 Commission excused our national leaders from any responsibility for the catastrophe. Had there been accountability at the highest level of government in this instance, it could have prevented hurricane Katrina from being a full blown catastrophe.

The 9/11 Commission traded off accountability on one disaster and tens of thousands of others paid the price in another. Without accountability, the absence of preparedness and competence did repeat itself at the time of Katrina. When enacting future investigative commissions Congress should require accountability through the highest levels of government.

Structuring Future Investigative Commissions

The 9/11 experience has shown us that investigative commissions can be politicized, no matter how able their members are, and especially when a very intense presidential election is underway. Members of future investigative commissions should be selected based on their broad expertise in the subject area and analytical ability. They should not be retired politicians who are vulnerable, as the 9/11 members were, to a politicized result. They should not be put in the predicament of having to decide matters of national importance in conflict with their deeply-held party loyalty.

It should be noted that a fifty-fifty political split on the Commission did not protect the public interest in this case. Rather, it almost assured a standoff on what was the pivotal issue – U.S. preparedness for the upcoming attacks.

Informing Congress and the Public of Imminent Threats

Unfortunately, by keeping silent the President made it easy for the 9/11 attackers to succeed. As we have seen public knowledge of an impending domestic threat has been one of our best defenses. Congress should modify the War Powers Act to require that, when credible information exists on an imminent domestic attack, the president must inform the public and consult with Congress on necessary precautions.

———

ENDNOTES

A few members of the Bush national security team and the 9/11 Commission were given an opportunity to comment on much of the material in this chapter and did not respond. The Terror Timeline book has many hundreds of sources and is the best guide for what the Bush administration actually knew about al-Qaeda's intentions before 9/11. It and many other reliable sources below can be found on the Internet.

1. "U.S. never had firm grip on terrorism," Judith Miller, Jeff Gerth and Don Van Natta Jr., *New York Times*.
2. "The Secret History," *Time Magazine*, August 12, 2002, p. 32.
3. "Broad Effort Launched After '98 Attack," Barton Gellman, *Washington Post*, December 19, 2001.
4. Ibid
5. "The Secret History," *Time Magazine*, August 12, 2002, p. 31.
6. "Against All Enemies," Richard Clarke, *Free Press*, 2004, p. 230.
7. "A Strategy of Cautious Evolution," Barton Gellman, *Washington Post,* Jan. 20, 2002. Angler – The Cheney Vice-Presidency (Chapter Five), Barton Gellman, Penguin books, 2008.
8. "The Secret History," *Time Magazine*, August 12, 2002.

9. "We Predicted It," Jake Tapper, *Salon*, September 12, 2001. "A Strategy of Cautious Evolution," Barton Gellman, *Washington Post*, Jan. 20, 2002. Angler – The Cheney Vice-Presidency (Chapter Five), Barton Gellman, Penguin books, 2008.

10. "In early '01, Bremer Bashed Bush on Terror," Kevin Featherly, Kevlog Archive, April 29, 2004. "Paul Bremer chaired the Congressionally created National Commission on Terrorism and issued his report in June 2000. There is no evidence of a meaningful response by the Executive Branch." See also The Terror Timeline, Regan Books, 2004, p. 90.

11. "A Strategy of Cautious Evolution," Barton Gellman, *Washington Post*, Jan. 20, 2002. Angler – The Cheney Vice-Presidency (Chapter Five), Barton Gellman, Penguin books, 2008.

12. Ibid

13. Ibid

14. The Terror Timeline: Year By Year, Day By Day, Minute By Minute, A Comprehensive Chronicle of the Road to 9/11 and America's Response, especially Part I, Chapter 1, Warning Signs and Chapter 3 Counterterrorism Before 9/11, Paul Thompson, Harper Collins, 2004. The information can also be found at http://www.historycommons.org, Complete 9/11 Timeline, Foreign Intelligence Agency Attack Warnings.

15. "Egypt Warned U.S. of an al-Qaeda Plot, Mubarak Asserts," Patrick Tyler and Neil MacFarquhar, *New York Times*, June 3, 2002.

16. "Joint Congressional inquiry into the intelligence community, December 20, 2002. America had 12 warnings of aircraft attack," Rupert Cornwell, Independent.co.uk, Sept. 19, 2002.

17. The 9/11 Commission Report, especially Executive Summary and Chapter on "The System Is Blinking Red," July 22, 2004.

18. Ibid

19. Ibid

20. Ibid

21. State of Denial, Bob Woodward, Simon & Schuster, 2006 (pp. 49-52 and 79-80).

22. Ibid

24. "The Secret History," *Time Magazine,* August 12, 2002.

25. Pre-Attack Memo Cited Bin Laden, David Johnston, *New York Times*, May, 2002. Tenet's visits to Crawford August 2001, Fred Kaplan and Soflalady, Democratic Underground.com, April 17, 2004.

26. The 9/11 Commission Report, "Executive Summary" and Chapter on "The System Is Blinking Red," July 22, 2004.

27. "The Secret History," *Time Magazine*, August 12, 2002.

28. The 9/11 Commission Report, Chapter on "The System Is Blinking Red," July 22, 2004. "'01 Memo to Rice Warned of Qaeda and Offered Plan," Scott Shane, *New York Times*, February 12, 2005.

29. "Ashcroft Flying High," *CBS News*, July 26, 2001.

30. The 9/11 Commission Report, Chapter on "The System Is Blinking Red," July 22, 2004.

31. "A Strategy of Cautious Evolution," Barton Gellman, *Washington Post*, Jan. 20, 2002. Angler – The Cheney Vice-Presidency (Chapter Five), Barton Gellman, Penguin Books, 2008.

32. The 9/11 Commission Report, Chapter on "The System Is Blinking Red," July 22, 2004.

33. Ibid

34. "Rumsfeld remains largely unapologetic in memoir," Bradley Graham, *Washington Post*, Feb. 3, 2011.

35. "The Book on Terror," David Ignatius, *Washington Post*, July 30, 2004.

36. Angler – The Cheney Vice-Presidency (Chapter Five), Barton Gellman, Penguin Books, 2008.

37. Ibid

38. The 9/11 Commission Report, Chapter on "The System Is Blinking Red," July 22, 2004.

39. Ibid

40. Ibid

41. State of Denial, Bob Woodward, 2006 (pp. 49-52 and 79-80).

42. The Terror Timeline: Year By Year, Day By Day, Minute By Minute, A Comprehensive Chronicle of the Road to 9/11 and America's Response, especially Part I, Chapter 1, "Warning Signs and Chapter 3 Counterterrorism Before 9/11," Paul Thompson, Harper Collins, 2004. The information can also be found at http://www.historycommons.org, Complete 9/11 Timeline, Foreign Intelligence Agency Attack Warnings.

43. "The Secret History," Time Magazine, August 12, 2002.

44. Angler – The Cheney Vice-Presidency (Chapter Five), Barton Gellman, Penguin Books, 2008. "Investigating the Investigation," Morton Mintz, *AlterNet*, Feb. 10, 2004.

45. "9/11 Panel Threatens to Issue Subpoena for Bush's Briefings," *New York Times*, February 10, 2004. Below are some of the other articles dealing with the White House cover-up.

　　"White House refuses to release September 11 info," *Knight Ridder Newspapers*, May 5, 2003.

　　"White House keeps secrets to hide failure, Graham says" *Palm Beach Post*, 2003.

　　"Sept. 11 panel criticizes White House," *Los Angeles Times*, July 9, 2003;

　　"Why does 9/11 inquiry scare Bush," *The Berkshire Eagle*, July 12, 2003.

　　"Sept. 11 panel leader warns White House of subpoenas," *The New York Times*, October 26, 2003.

　　"Stonewalling the 9/11 Commission," *Wall Street Journal*, July 8, 2003.

　　"9/11 Panel Seeks More Documents From White House," *Washington Post*, September 24, 2003.

　　"9/11 Panel May Reject Offer of Limited Access to Briefings," *New York Times*, November 7, 2003.

　　"Sept. 11 panelists, victim's families rip document deal," *New York Times*, November 14, 2003.

　　"The 9/11 Cover-up," AlterNet.org, November 21, 2003.

　　"9/11 family statement re: Commission access to sensitive documents and conflict of interest," *Voices of September 11 Newsletter* December 2, 2003.

　　"What's Bush Hiding from 9/11 Commission?," *Working for Change*, January 22, 2004.

　　"Sept. 11 Commission Faces Fight Over Deadline Extension," *Gov Exec,* January 21, 2004.

　　"White House Holding Notes Taken by 9/11 Commission," *Washington Post*, January 31, 2004.

"The White House: A New Fight Over Sept. 11," *Newsweek*, February 10, 2004.

"9/11 Panel to Accept Summary of Briefings," *Washington Post*, February 11, 2004.

"Failure of 9/11 Commission to Subpoena the White House," *Voices of September 11 Newsletter*, February 11, 2004.

"Bush Plays Bait-and-Switch with 9/11 Panel," *Newsday.com*, February 19, 2004.

Statement of 9/11 Families on commission access to presidential daily briefings, extension of its deadline and request for Senate hearings on progress, February 20, 2004.

46. Ibid.

47. The Emperor's New Clothes – Exposing The Truth From Watergate to 9/11, Richard Ben-Veniste, St. Martin Press, June, 2009. "Bush Criticized By Former 9/11 Commission Member," Pete Yost, *Associated Press*, May 22, 2009.

48. "9/11 family statement re: Commission access to sensitive documents and conflict of interest," *Voices of September 11 Newsletter* December 2, 2003.

49. The 9/11 Commission Report, July 22, 2004.

50. "9/11 family statement re: Commission access to sensitive documents and conflict of interest," *Voices of September 11 Newsletter* December 2, 2003.

51. The Emperor's New Clothes – Exposing The Truth From Watergate to 9/11, Richard Ben-Veniste, St. Martin Press, June, 2009. "Bush Criticized By Former 9/11 Commission Member," Pete Yost, *Associated Press*, May 22, 2009.

52. "Pinning the Blame," Elisabeth Drew, *The New York Review of Books*, Sept. 23, 2004. Drew reached a similar conclusion as in this book, based on her close reading of the Commission report and interviews with Commissioners and key staff members.

53. The 9/11 Commission Report, "Executive Summary" and Chapter on "The System Is Blinking Red," July 22, 2004.

54. Ibid.

55. Ibid.

56. "Pinning the Blame", Elisabeth Drew, *The New York Review of Books*, Sept. 23, 2004. Drew reached a similar conclusion as this book based on her close reading of the Commission report and interviews with Commissioners and key staff members.
57. The Emperor's New Clothes – Exposing The Truth From Watergate to 9/11, Richard Ben-Veniste, St. Martin Press, June, 2009.
58. Film, *9/11: Press for Truth* (on internet). Co-produced by Rory O'Connor and Kyle Hence with Globalvision and inputs from 9/11 widows and Paul Thompson, author of The Time Line.
59. "President Bush saved U.S. lives? That's only more Karl Rove-style spin," Richard Clarke, *N.Y. Daily News*, Jan. 8, 2009. "Trauma of 9/11 Is No Excuse," Richard Clarke, *Washington Post*, May 21, 2009.
60. Ibid.
61. The 9/11 Commission Report, Chapter on "The System Is Blinking Red," July 22, 2004.
62. Ibid.
63. "Pre-Attack Memo Cited Bin Laden," David Johnston, *New York Times*, May, 2002. "Tenet's visits to Crawford August 2001," Fred Kaplan and Soflalady, *Democratic Underground.com*, April 17, 2004.
64. Two separate 9/11 Widows' statements object to mistakes of the 9/11 Commission: "An Open Letter to Senator Leahy," *Buzzflash*, Mar. 3, 2009 and "Response to Xmas Day Terror Attempt," *Opednews.com*, Jan. 8, 2010.

OTHER RELATED SOURCES

"The Secrets of September 11," *MSNBC.com*, May 1, 2003.

"Terror Commission Seeks Classified Papers," Associated Press, February 28, 2003.

"Why keep Americans guessing about 9/11?" *Sacramento Bee*, May 16, 2003.

"Classified: Censoring the Report About 9/11?" Michael Isikoff, *Newsweek,* June 1, 2002.

"9/11 Report Cites Intelligence Failures," *Associated Press*, July 24, 2003.

"The 9/11 Report Raises More Questions about the White House Statements on Intelligence," John Dean, *Find Law's Legal Commentary*, July 29, 2003.

"Where the Blame Lies," *Intervention Magazine*, December 11, 2003.

"Clarke blaming Bush for not taking precautions before World Trade Center attack," *Foster's/Citizen Online*, December 11, 2003.

"Condi and the 9/11 Commission," *Time Online Edition*, December 23, 2003.

"September 11: Will Terror Panel's Report Be an Election Issue?" *Newsweek*, January 14, 2004.

"Bush agrees to New 9/11 Commission Deadline," *Associated Press*, February 5, 2004.

Voices of September 11 Newsletter, February 9, 2004.

"White House Noncommittal on Testimony," *Palm Beach Post*, February 13, 2004.

"President Agrees to Meet (Part of) Panel Privately About September 11 Attacks," *Palm Beach Post*, February 14, 2004.

"Weak on Terror," *New York Times*, March 16, 2004.

"Bush and 9/11: What We Need to Know," *Time Magazine*, March 17, 2004.

Statement of 9/11 families on Condoleezza Rice Testimony, March 30, 2004.

"9/11 Widows," *New York Times*, April 1, 2004.

"Uneven Response Seen on Terror in Summer of 2001," *New York Times*, April 4, 2004.

"Declassified Memo Said al-Qaeda Was in U.S.," *Washington Post*, April 10, 2004.

"The Texas Try on Terrorism," *Center For American Progress*, April 12, 2004.

"The 9/11 Investigation: Bending Reality," *St. Louis Post Dispatch*, April 12, 2004.

"Will Bush Own Up?" *Washington Post*, April 13, 2004.

"Panel Says Bush Saw Repeated Warnings," *Washington Post*, April 14, 2004.

"9/11 Files Show Warnings Were Urgent and Persistent," *New York Times*, April 18, 2004.

"The Wrong Debate on Terrorism," Richard Clarke, *New York Times*, April 25, 2004.

"Will The Commissioners Cave?" *Tom Paine Common Sense*, June 21, 2004.

"Report on 9/11 to be released this month," *Knight Ridder*, July 10, 2004.

"Correcting the record on 9/11," *New York Times*.

"9/11 Panel Roiling Campaign Platforms," *Washington Post*, August 9, 2004.

"9/11 Assessment Again Shows Lost Personal Responsibility," *The Boston Channel*, August 10, 2004.

"We could have stopped him," *Guardian Unlimited*, August 10, 2004.

"Former CIA Agent Says Bush to Blame for 9/11," *Common Dreams*, September 22, 2004.

"The 9/11 Secret in the CIA's Back Pocket," *Los Angeles Times*, October 19, 2004.

"Evolving Nature of al-Qaeda Is Misunderstood Critic Says," *New York Times*, November 8, 2004.

"Bush team tried to suppress pre-9/11 report into al-Qaeda, Andrew Buncombe," *The Independent*, February 11, 2005

"Revealed: The Taliban minister, the U.S. envoy and the warning of September 11 that was ignored, Kate Clark in Kabul," *The Independent*, Sept. 7, 2002.

"Plane Attacks Seen as Threat Before Sept. 11," Rebecca Carr, *Palm Beach Post Washington Bureau*, Sept. 19, 2002.

"Bush briefed on hijacking threat before September 11," John King, *CNN Washington Bureau. CNN.com.*

"Israeli security issued urgent warnings to CIA of large-scale terror attacks," David Wastell and Philip Jacobson, *The Telegraph*, October 8, 2002.

Chapter Three

LAUNCHING TWO NEEDLESS WARS

"President Bush was anxious to go to war in Iraq because he had been 'caught with his pants down.' Although the CIA got the blame for 9/11, the White House had been warned numerous times and simply didn't respond."

Pulitzer Prize journalist Thomas Ricks on NBC's Meet the Press

War in Afghanistan

Following the 9/11 catastrophe the right wing administration hurriedly implemented the attack plan it had ignored earlier that was passed on by the previous administration. This plan called for CIA covert personnel, the U.S. military and the Northern Alliance to put an end to the al-Qaeda network in Afghanistan. The plan went well except that the administration allowed Bin Laden and members of his network to escape into Pakistan and did not pursue them.

At that point the administration had two options and adopted neither: (1) have the Pakistan government dismantle the al-Qaeda network that had entered its own country—with or without U.S assistance—or (2) simply use elite U.S. Special Forces to get the job done as a matter of America's **self defense**.

No country has the right to harbor an international terrorist network whose obvious purpose is to undermine other governments and kill innocent civilians. There would have been worldwide support at the time for a full and complete U.S. response to the 9/11 attacks.

Instead of finishing the job, the administration decided to set up a new government in Afghanistan, using military force. That meant military occupation and taking control of the country—something no other foreign military force in history had done successfully. The administration then doomed its own strategy to failure by diverting U.S. military forces to an invasion of Iraq, and still another occupation.

Rather than take ownership of the country, the U.S. should have dropped millions of leaflets over Afghanistan notifying the government and its people of the extraordinary response we would make if they ever again permitted a safe haven for international terrorism of any kind.

There was no need to go to war. The killing of Bin Laden ten years later in Pakistan did not require an invasion or military occupation. The same would have been true earlier.

Former Defense Secretary Gates has since acknowledged that an American land war in Asia, the Mideast or Africa is foolhardy. [1] The next chapter will discuss further the Afghanistan war in the context of (1) the War Powers Act and (2) a more effective U.S. policy for international terrorism.

War in Iraq

Within fifteen days after 9/11, the President called Defense Secretary Rumsfeld to the White House and ordered a review and revision of war plans for Iraq. [2] As Bob Woodward describes in detail in his book, Plan of Attack, Bush had decided on a path to war well over a year before the invasion. A photo in Woodward's book shows the President meeting with General Tommy Franks in Crawford, Texas on Dec. 28, 2001, for a "war planning session on Iraq."

At the President's direction, the CIA participated in this war planning and sent a team to northern Iraq to lay the groundwork for the invasion. To arrange for its covert entry, CIA Director Tenet personally went there in March 2002 (a year before the actual invasion) and told Iraqi Kurd leaders that the United States was serious—the military and the CIA were coming.

In mid-2002, President Bush shifted $700 million from the Afghanistan war to preparations for war in Iraq. By then, the inevitably of Bush's war became clear in the now famous British Downing Street memo.[3] The secret Downing Street meeting concluded that:

- Military action was inevitable—Bush had made up his mind.
- Intelligence and facts were being fixed around the policy.
- Military action would begin January 2003 (actually March 2003).
- The case was thin—Saddam was not threatening his neighbors and his weapon of mass destruction (WMD) capability was less than those of Libya, North Korea, and Iran.
- The White House had no patience with going through the United Nations to achieve its ends.
- There was little discussion of the aftermath following military action.
- Prime Minister Blair concluded that it would make a big difference politically and legally if Saddam refused to let the UN inspectors back in. (Saddam did not refuse).

During the summer and fall of 2002, Administration officials went public and referred to ominous Iraq Weapons of Mass Destruction, linked Iraq to al-Qaeda, and speculated about the possibility of another catastrophe like 9/11. The result was a policy-based decision that drove the intelligence, rather than the other way around. Adding to this pressure, the White House gave the CIA only three weeks to prepare an October 2002 *National Intelligence Estimate* for Congress to authorize the use of force.

Never a Case for War

Defense Secretary Rumsfeld made numerous public statements declaring he was certain of WMDs in Iraq. For example in mid September 2002, he said "There's no doubt in the world as to whether they have those weapons ... we all know that. A trained ape knows that." Earlier that month, however, his Director of Intelligence for the Joint Chiefs of Staff reported to him that our intelligence was filled with uncertainties and lack of "hard evidence" about the existence of such weapons.[4]

Meanwhile, people inside the CIA were "disheartened, dispirited, and angry." One senior CIA official put it this way, "Information not consistent with the Administration agenda was discarded and information that was [consistent] was not seriously scrutinized." As war approached, U.S. intelligence analysts were questioning almost every major piece of WMD intelligence.[5] The CIA chief weapons inspector, David Kay, sent to Iraq after the invasion to locate WMDs, had this comment on the earlier CIA work:

"Anything that showed Iraq didn't have weapons of mass destruction had a much higher gate to pass because if it were true, all U.S. policy towards Iraq would have fallen asunder."[6]

The CIA Ombudsman told Congress that the Administration's "hammering" of the CIA was harder than he had seen in his thirty-two years at the agency. In addition to the pressure on CIA analysts to go along, top policymakers sought, and selectively used, raw intelligence data to support their case.

As Seymour Hersh reported in *The New Yorker* Magazine, this raw data was not exposed to the vigorous scrutiny traditionally followed in the intelligence community. Bypassing this scrutiny is known as "stovepiping."[7]

The raw data included some information furnished by Iraqi defectors and exile groups, who were actively promoting an American invasion of Iraq. Questionable intelligence from these various sources found a receptive audience among Defense Department policymakers and in the Vice-President's office.

Later, key members of the Senate Select Committee on Intelligence (Senators Levin, Durbin and Rockefeller) concluded that:

- **"As invasion plans were readied and finalized, the Administration had succeeded in painting a stark and sobering picture of an imminent threat to American security based on fragmentary intelligence and overheated rhetoric. The Vice President had** told a nationwide television audience that Iraq not only had a nuclear weapons development program but had, in fact, reconstituted nuclear weapons.

- **"The President spoke of a 'mushroom cloud' and 'massive and sudden horror,' while top officials continued to link Iraq and al-Qaeda terrorism in vivid terms that went well beyond what the Intelligence Community assessed."**[8]

After the invasion, Senator Bill Nelson made public what had transpired in a secret Senate briefing before the war. In this secret briefing, Vice-President Cheney and the CIA Director told Senators that Saddam could deliver biological and chemical weapons (notably anthrax) to our cities along the eastern seaboard using aerial pilotless vehicles.

The Senate had already dealt with a horrible anthrax scare right after 9/11 and naturally feared another. Before the invasion, however, our own Air Force and U.N. inspectors on the ground in Iraq had already determined that these pilotless vehicles were probably designed for only reconnaissance missions.[9]

None of the twenty-odd claims in Secretary Powell's U.N. presentation have been borne out. Powell's presentation depended on artist conceptions and simulation of the threat. To increase the impact, he held a simulated vial of anthrax in his hand for the world to see. Meanwhile, Secretary Rumsfeld claimed at press briefings that he, in fact, knew the exact location in Iraq of two WMD sites.[10]

The U.N. had sent 250 international inspectors to Iraq to obtain the actual facts. The inspectors were impartial, professional weapons inspectors from some sixty countries around the world. They made 700 inspections at 500 sites. They had no axe to grind. Our own weapon experts were invited to participate in the inspections, but the administration declined.

Dr. El Baradei headed the nuclear team and Hans Blix headed the team on other weapons. Dr. El Baradei was Director General of the International Atomic Energy Agency and later received a Nobel Prize for his work in the nuclear field.

The inspectors eventually got cooperation from Iraq and, despite several tip-offs from American and British intelligence, found no evidence of a nuclear program or of chemical/biological weapons. Their preliminary findings were reported to the U.N. publicly in January and March 2003. They discounted U.S. intelligence and their findings should have prevented war.

Dr. El Baradei's briefing to the U.N. Security Council also challenged U.S. allegations on Iraq acquiring (1) uranium from Niger and (2) aluminum tubes for enriching uranium. Inspections ended soon thereafter when the President decided to invade Iraq. The arms inspectors wanted more time, but the invasion put them out of business.[11]

Several weeks before the invasion, Germany appealed to the U.S. not to go to war. A member of their foreign ministry flew to Washington and met strong resistance from the White House. The German view was that the political costs of war were too high, the beneficiary would be Iran, war would precipitate a "terrorist backlash" and it would further complicate reaching a solution to the Israeli/Palestinian conflict.

Germany thought the inspectors on the ground should be given more time. In this last minute attempt to avert war, Germany had the support of both Russia and France.

Dr. El Baradei has since accused U.S. leaders of "grotesque distortions" in claiming Iraq possessed doomsday weapons despite contrary information collected by him and other arms inspectors inside the country. He believes that the International Criminal Court should investigate whether U.S. leaders committed a war crime.[12]

Working in the Climate of Impending War

It was common knowledge that the CIA did not have a good network of sources in Iraq. The source on mobile biological weapons was a suspected fabricator in Germany who was considered mentally unstable.[13] He later told the UK Guardian newspaper, "They gave me this chance ... to fabricate something to topple the regime."

A later investigative commission found that (1) doubts about the intelligence existed within the CIA and other agencies, but they were dismissed and (2) intelligence analysts were working in a climate of "impending war" that did not encourage skepticism.[14] For example:

- Analysts were forced to complete their work for Congress in a three-week time frame.
- Intense policymaker interest contributed to willingness to accept dubious claims and an unwillingness to reject them.
- The climate shifted the burden of proof from proving that illegal weapons existed to proving that they did not exist.
- Neither analysts nor users were open to being told that evidence supporting the assumptions was uncertain or unreliable.
- Analysts thought war was inevitable before they finished their work.

In an explosive and informative 2007 documentary, former experts from the CIA, Pentagon and Foreign Service explained how the White House pressured the CIA to conform to the Administration's desires and misled the nation into war. The experts said "CIA intelligence was circumstantial and inferential ... and always with qualifications."

They said there was intervention into the operations of the CIA, especially by the Vice-President's office. They said it was unethical and immoral for the Administration to constantly connect Iraq to 9/11 and to a "mushroom cloud" nuclear program, when there was no real evidence of either.[15]

A year after the Iraq invasion, an Army War College report concluded:

- Saddam had been deterred and did not present a threat.
- Taking him down was a distraction from the war on terror.
- The anti-terror campaign is unfocused and threatens to dissipate U.S. military resources.
- The U.S. Army is "near the breaking point."[16]

Other Reasons to Declare War Were Unjustified

Once the major claims of WMDs made in the build-up to war were discredited, the Bush administration began to put out various other reasons for going to war:

1. Saddam eventually would have converted facilities from civilian to Weapons' production, reconstituted his former programs, and passed weapons on to al-Qaeda terrorists.

There are three problems with this scenario: First, the President got America's support on the grounds that Iraq was concealing lethal weapons and was an immediate threat to the United States and the region. Support would have evaporated had the President's case for war been based on assumptions of some remote threat in the future. And, it's extremely doubtful that the White House would have even proposed such a weak war authorization to Congress.

Second, possible conversion of civilian facilities to weapons use is not sufficient reason to justify war. In fact, war could be started on this basis in many parts of the world and at any time.

Third, Iraq was not **then** a terrorist state. Dr. Kay's huge inspection team looking for WMDs after the invasion found no evidence of transfers of illegal weapons to terrorists.[17] The administration ordered CIA analysts, repeatedly, to redo intelligence assessments to show an Iraqi connection with the al-Qaeda network, but the analysts refused to alter their conclusions.[18] Later, the 9/11 Commission backed them up.

2. Iraq is now the central front for the war on terrorism.

Iraq had little to do with terrorism until we made it so, by invading a Muslim nation based on false premises. There were rumors of an al-Qaeda training camp in the Kurdish north, but that part of Iraq was not under Saddam's control.

3. If we don't fight the terrorists in Iraq now, we will have to fight them one day in the streets of American cities.

This is pure conjecture and would have not been grounds for Congress to authorize war. There was no serious problem with international terrorism in Iraq until we invaded that country. It is far more likely that an unprovoked invasion of a Muslim country inspired resistance by Iraqi citizens and attracted terrorist groups around the globe resenting our military intrusion.

4. The war was justified "because we removed a regime that did have these weapons and gave us no reason to believe they had eliminated them."

"Did" is the operative word. In order to avoid a preemptive war, does a country have to prove a negative? Poor Iraqi bookkeeping (documented destruction of weapons) does not justify war. In any event, international weapons experts were there on the ground discovering the truth and that information should have been used.

5. The world is a safer/better place without Saddam.

Actually, Saddam had been defanged before the war. Containing him had worked. His regime was slowly crumbling under U.N. sanctions and no-fly zones. Both Secretary of State Powell and National Security Advisor Rice said publicly in 2001 that Saddam posed no threat.

6. Congress and countries around the world also believed Saddam had WMD's.

The President contends that the whole world was fooled about Saddam's weapons. According to German intelligence people, the Bush Administration repeatedly exaggerated its intelligence on Iraq's biological weapons – despite multiple warnings questioning its reliability. Similarly, the French challenged U.S. intelligence on Saddam's nuclear program.[19] As noted earlier, Germany, France and Russia wanted the U.S. to delay its invasion until the international inspectors in Iraq had completed their work.

Smaller countries, like Germany and France, neither have the big budget nor extensive military intelligence apparatus that we do. But, whatever they believed, they had enough sense to hold out for the facts before agreeing to sign on to a preemptive war. These stubborn facts were becoming available from onsite inspections, but were being ignored by our right-wing administration.

7. Congress had access to the same intelligence data that the President did.

Not true. By virtue of his role as Commander-in-Chief, the President had far greater access to volumes of intelligence and sensitive information, such as sources and methods. In this case, Congress only got a summarized, sanitized version without all the dissents and caveats.

Politicians and people in the media have used this same excuse. As will be explained in Chapter Seven, Congress and the media didn't do their job. Instead, they relied too heavily on statements of the President, Vice-President and Secretary of Defense. The media simply wanted to tag along (get permission to be imbedded with U.S. troops) and report the war from there.

Since Bush was dragging the American people into war against the advice of much of the world community, it was his responsibility to get the facts straight and be sure of his position.

8. We needed to spread democracy throughout the Mideast.

As a Muslim Nobel prize winner said, "democracy is a historical process and cannot be imposed militarily from the outside." The CIA, State Department, and an international consulting firm all warned the Administration about the difficulties of trying to build democracy "on the ashes of Saddam's regime."[20]

An Iraqi woman in Baghdad, who has drawn worldwide respect for her reporting on the personal hardships and daily lives of Iraqis, had this to say about spreading democracy:

"Democracy has to come from within and it has to be a request of the people—not of expatriates who have alliances with the CIA and British intelligence. People have to want something enough to rise up and change it. They have to be ready for democracy and willing to accept its responsibility. The U.S. could have promoted democracy peacefully."[21]

Many of our Presidents of the past have tried to promote and assist other countries in achieving democracy, but never by military force. The Bush right-wing administration chose the wrong way to spread freedom and, as will be discussed in the next chapter, the wrong way to counter international terrorism.

Conclusions and Remedies

By staging a unilateral, preemptive war based on bad information, the Bush right-wing administration has opened Pandora's Box. We have set a horrible precedent. It is taking years to repair America's credibility and rebuild trust in our Government.

Vice-President Cheney had served both in Congress and in several administrations, including positions as White House Chief of Staff and Secretary of Defense. He knew first hand that threat assessments are based on estimates and assumptions, sometimes using questionable sources. Yet, both he and the President presented this information over and over again to the public with absolute certainty. Then, as the 2002 midterm elections approached, the President and Vice-President intimidated Congress into passing open-ended authority, allowing use of force in Iraq.

When the President sought authority to use force, he promised Congress and the American people that he would not engage in war, except as a last resort. He did not fulfill that promise and continued to use threat information that is inherently uncertain.

At the very least, the Administration should have let the international inspectors finish their work and check out the dissents and caveats of our intelligence community. Unfortunately, the U.S. invasion forced the inspectors to leave.

These inspectors had already reported no evidence of a nuclear program and were disproving other U.S. data on biological and chemical weapons.[22] They wanted more time, but the administration wanted war.

Aside from misusing faulty intelligence, the President and Vice-President continually misled the public and Congress into believing that Saddam had some connection with 9/11. They spoke as if they actually knew about the connection whereas the CIA had repeatedly told them that there was no support for this proposition.[23]

The President and his advisors were already on a path to war and used intelligence to suit their own needs. Had the President taken normal precautions, it would have been evident before the war that (1) U.S. intelligence was suspect, (2) his assertions to Congress and the public about the threat were incorrect, and (3) these assertions were at that very time being disproved by inspectors on the ground in Iraq.

President Bush's tone, in his public utterances, was that his noble objective of advancing freedom will somehow absolve him of the many mistakes he made during the lead up to war and during the military occupation. History will not be so kind. And, historians will wonder whether terrorist attacks around the world would have escalated as much as they did if the United States had not gone precipitously to war against a country that posed no threat.

Later, the Senate Intelligence Committee launched an inquiry into this matter. But, as in the case of the 9/11 Commission investigation, presidential politics got in the way (See chapter2). The right-wing Committee Chairman deferred dealing with that portion of the inquiry on how the White House had used and influenced pre-war intelligence until after the election. Then, he quietly abandoned it.

Consequently, the American people had to decide on a President's reelection without having crucial information on his performance at a critical moment in our history. The same thing happened earlier on 9/11 as a result of a cover-up by the White House and the 9/11 Commission. The media was too weak to confront the cover-ups (See chapter seven).

When a nation is in fear of attack and there is heavily cloaked national security information, it is difficult to stop a determined president from going to war. This is especially true at reelection time when members of Congress may fear losing their jobs for appearing to be unpatriotic.

The War Powers Act needs to be modified to require, except in immediate national emergencies, that Congress hold hearings with the executive on:

- Alternatives to war,
- Alternatives to military occupation, and
- Alternative exit strategies, if we go to war.

The next chapter discusses other important changes to the War Powers Act.

———

ENDNOTES

1. "Gates Warns Against More Wars Like Iraq and Afghanistan," Thorn Shanker, *Truthout*, Feb. 25, 2011.
2. "Bush, Rumsfeld and Iraq: Is the Real Reason for the Invasion Finally Emerging?" *Truthout*, Feb. 6, 2011.
3. "The Secret Downing Street Memo, David Manning," *The Sunday Times-Britain*, May 1, 2005.
4. "Simply the Worst," Maureen Dowd, *New York Times*, Feb. 12, 2011. "Rumsfeld Memoir: Known and Unknown and Untrue," David Corn and Siddhartha, *Mother Jones*, Feb. 8, 2011.
5. "CIA shapes intelligence data to meet administration policy goals," *Washington Post*, June 12, 2003; "Ex-Spies: CIA Workers Outraged," *CBS news.com*, July 19, 2003; "Prewar Findings Worried Analysts" Walter Pincus, *Washington Post*, May 22, 2005.
6. "Kay Report/No WMD, No Case for War," *Star Tribune*, Oct. 4, 2003; Dr. Kay's testimony and public statements, January/February 2004.
7. "The Stovepipe," Seymour Hersh, *New Yorker*, October 27, 2003.
8. "Additional Views Of Rockefeller, Levin and Durbin," Report on the U.S. Intelligence Community's Prewar Intelligence Assessments On Iraq, Select Committee On Intelligence, U.S. Senate, July 7, 2004.
9. "Senators were told Iraqi weapons could hit U.S. Florida," *Today. com*, December 15, 2003; "Prewar Findings Worried Analysts" Walter Pincus, *Washington Post*, May 22, 2005.
10. "Rumsfeld Memoir: Known and Unknown and Untrue," David Corn and Siddhartha, *Mother Jones*, Feb. 8, 2011.
11. "Hans Blix Says Iraq War Was Unfounded," *Guardian Unlimited*, Feb. 24, 2004. "Blix states Iraq war was illegal," *Nettanisen*, March 5, 2004. "Panel: U.S. Ignored Work of U.N. Arms Inspectors," Dafna Linzer,

Washington Post, April 3, 2005. *9/11 Commission Report*, such as page 59 and footnotes 72 and 299. Inspection reports on the U.N. website (Briefings of UNMOVIC and IAEA to the U.N. on March 7, 2003). "Now They Tell Us," *The New York Review of Books*, February 26, 2004, pp. 10-18; "Prewar Findings Worried Analysts," Walter Pincus, *Washington Post*, May 22, 2005.

12. "Berlin Efforts to Prevent Iraq War Invasion," Klaus Wiegrefe, *Stiegel Online*, Nov. 24, 2010. "El Baradei suggests war crimes probe of Bush team," Charles Hanley, AP Special Correspondent, April 22, 2011.

13. The Commission on the Intelligence Capabilities of the United States Regarding Weapons of Mass Destruction, Biological Warfare Finding 4, March 31, 2005.

14. *The Commission on the Intelligence Capabilities of the United States Regarding Weapons of Mass Destruction*, Biological Warfare Findings 3 and 4, Conclusions 12, 24, and 26, March 31, 2005. "A Final Verdict on Prewar Intelligence Is Still Elusive," Todd Purdum, *New York Times*, April 1, 2005.

15. *UNCOVERED Documentary, The Whole Truth About the Iraq War*, Robert Greenwald, 2007. Infighting among U.S. intelligence fuels dispute over Iraq, Warren Strobel and Jonathan Landay, McClatchy Washington Bureau, Oct. 24, 2002.

16. "Study Published by Army Criticizes War on Terror's Scope", *Washington Post*, Jan. 12, 2004.

17. "Kay Report/No WMD, No Case for War," *Star Tribune*, Oct. 4, 2003; Dr. Kay's testimony and public statements, January/Febuary 2004.

18. "Questions Grow Over Iraq Links to al-Qaeda," Peter Canellos and Bryon Bender, *Boston Globe*, August 3, 2003; "CIA Felt Pressure to Alter Iraq Data, Author Says," *Common Dreams New Center*, July 1, 2004; "CIA Finds No Evidence Hussein Sought to Arm Terrorists," *Washington Post*, November 16, 2003.

19. "Who Forged the Niger Documents?" Ian Masters, *AlterNet.org*, April 7, 2005.

20. "Nobel winner says U.S. cannot impose democracy," *Reuters*, June 3, 2004. "Democracy Might Be Impossible, U.S. Was Told," *Boston Globe*, August 14, 2003.

21. Buzzflash interview with a Baghdad blogger, April 15, 2005.
22. "Hans Blix Says Iraq War Was Unfounded," *Guardian Unlimited*, Feb. 24, 2004. "Blix states Iraq war was illegal" Nettanisen, March 5, 2004. "8 Panel: U.S. Ignored Work of U.N. Arms Inspectors," Dafna Linzer, *Washington Post*, April 3, 2005. *9/11 Commission Report*, such as page 59 and footnotes 72 and 299. Inspection reports on the U.N. website (Briefings of UNMOVIC and IAEA to the U.N. on March 7, 2003). "Now They Tell Us," *The New York Review of Books*, February 26, 2004, pp. 10-18; "Prewar Findings Worried Analysts," Walter Pincus, *Washington Post*, May 22, 2005.
23. "Questions Grow Over Iraq Links to al-Qaeda," Peter Canellos and Bryon Bender, *Boston Globe*, August 3, 2003; "CIA Felt Pressure to Alter Iraq Data, Author Says," *Common Dreams New Center*, July 1, 2004; "CIA Finds No Evidence Hussein Sought to Arm Terrorists," *Washington Post*, November 16, 2003.

OTHER RELATED SOURCES

"Report Says Iraq Is New Terrorist Training Ground," *Washington Post*, January 13, 2005.

"Bush asks millions as reward for allies," *Associated Press*, February 10, 2005.

"Report: al-Qaeda Ranks Swelling Worldwide," *Nation/World News*, May 26, 2004; "Al-Qaeda winning: Asian analysts" *The Age*, May 31, 2004.

"A State Department report disputes Bush's claim that ousting Hussein will spur reforms in the Mideast," *Los Angeles Times*, March 14, 2003.

"Democracy Domino Theory Not Credible," Greg Miller, *Los Angeles Times*, March 14, 2003.

"A reckless path," *The Washington Times*, Paul Craig Roberts, March 20, 2003.

"Hunt for Iraqi Arms Erodes Assumptions," *Washington Post*, April 22, 2003.

"Assessing the Weapons Search," *New York Times*, April 26, 2003.

"Revealed: How the road to war was paved with lies," *Independent.co.uk*, April 27, 2003.

"The Most Dangerous President Ever," *The American Prospect*, May 1, 2003.

"Neoconservative clout seen in U.S. policy," *Milwaukee Journal Sentinel*, May 10, 2003.

"Karl Rove's Campaign Strategy: It's the Terror," *New York Times*, May 10, 2003.

"Frustrated, U.S. Arms Team to Leave Iraq," *Washington Post*, May 11, 2003.

"Bush Officials Change Tune on Iraqi Weapons," *Reuters*, May 14, 2003.

"WMD just a convenient excuse for war," admits Wolfowitz, *Independent. co.uk*, May 30, 2003.

"Iraq repercussions trouble top advisors," *The Mercury News*, May 31, 2003.

"Truth and consequences," *US NEWS.com*, June 3, 2003.

John Dean articles dissecting the President's State of the Union speech, *Find Law's Legal Commentary*, June 6 and July 18, 2003.

"Ex-Official: Evidence Distorted for War," *Associated Press*, June 8, 2003.

"Bush's deception on Iraqi intelligence," *The Boston Globe*, June 8, 2003

"Reasons to Deceive," *Reuters*, June 18, 2003.

"CIA Officer: Bush Ignored Warnings," *Knight Ridder*, June 13, 2003.

"10 Appalling Lies We Were Told About Iraq," *AlterNet.org*, June 27, 2003.

"White House lied about Saddam threat," *Guardian Unlimited*, July 11, 2003.

"20 Lies about the War," *Independent.co.uk*, July 13, 2003.

"Pattern of Corruption," Paul Krugman, *New York Times*, July 15, 2003.

"Ten Questions for Cheney," *TomPaine.com*, July 22, 2003;

Full-page ads in 3 major newspapers challenging the honesty of the Bush administration, for example, *New York Times*, July 27, 2003.

"The Bush Administration's Top 40 lies About War and Terrorism," *CityPages.com*, July 30, 2003.

"Scientists Still Deny Iraqi Arms Programs," *Washington Post*, July 31, 2003.

"Prewar statements by Cheney under scrutiny," *Chicago Tribune*, August 6, 2003.

"Depiction of Threat Outgrew Supporting Evidence," Barton Gellman and Walter Pincus, *Washington Post*, August 10, 2003.

"U.S. Justification for War: How it Stacks Up Now," *Associated Press, Seattle Times*, August 10, 2003.

"Today we face another Watergate," *Newsday.com.*, August 11, 2003.

"The Bush Deceit," Peter Zimmerman, *Washington Post.com* August 14, 2003.

"A Price Too High," *New York Times*, August 21, 2003.

"AP Staffer Fact-Checks Powell's U.N. Speech....Key Claims Didn't Hold Up," *Editor & Publisher*, September 9, 2003.

"Will Press Roll Over Again on New WMD report?," *Editor & Publisher*, September 10, 2003.

Time Magazine Iraqi survey, October 6, 2003.

"Deception Down Under," *Tom Paine Common Sense*, October 14, 2003.

"Ex-Aide: Powell Misled Americans," *CBSNEWS.com*, October 15, 2003.

"Sen. Hagel Says Congress Deferred Too Much to Bush," *Washington Post*, October 21, 2003.

"No president has lied so badly and so often and so demonstrably," *Independent.co.uk*, November 19, 2003.

"War critics astonished as U.S. hawk admits invasion was illegal," *Guardian Unlimited*, November 26, 2003.

"Medical evacuations from Iraq near 11,000," *United Press International*, December 19, 2003.

"The Burden of Truth," *Sojourners*, December 20, 2003.

"Iraq's Arsenal Was Only on Paper," *Washington Post*, January 7, 2004.

"White House Distorted Iraq Threat," *Financial Times*, January 10, 2004.

"New WMD Report Slams Bush White House," *AlterNet.org*, January 13, 2004.

"Bush, Aides Ignored CIA Caveats on Iraq," *Washington Post*, February 7, 2004.

"The Use of Intelligence," *Boston Globe*, February 6, 2004.

Meet the Facts, Center for American Progress Report, February 9, 2004.

"Laurence Silberman: The Right Man or the Right's Man," Press Release, *People For The American Way*, February 13, 2004.

"British spy wrecked peace move," *Guardian Unlimited*, February 15, 2004.

"10% at Hospital Had Mental Problems," *Military.com*, February 19, 2004.

"Bush Wanted War in 2002," *Guardian Unlimited*, February 24, 2002.

"The Hollow Army," James Fallows, *The Atlantic*, March 2004.

Woodward, Bob, Plan of Attack, Simon & Schuster, 2004.

"U.S. admits the war for hearts and minds in Iraq is now lost," *Sunday Herald*, December 5, 2004.

"CIA Agent Says Bosses Ordered Him to Falsify WMD Reports," *Democracy Now*, December 16, 2004.

"Analysis: Only U.S. can damage self majorly despite bin Laden," *Associated Press*, December 18, 2004. [bin Laden bleeding superpowers]

"The Butcher's Bill, A look at the future of the war in Iraq," Jack Beatty, *Atlantic Unbound*, December 26, 2004.

"An army's morale on the downswing," William Pfaff, *International Herald Tribune*, December 29, 2004.

"Lauria Garret of Newsday Rips Tribune Co. Greed in Exit Memo," *Editor & Publisher*, March 1, 2005.

"Why Iraq Withdrawal Makes Sense," Norman Solomon, *Common Dreams News Center*, March 17, 2005.

"The coalition of the wilting", *Chicago Tribune*, March 21, 2005.

"M16, Jack Straw, defense staff: Blair ignored them all," John Ware, *Guardian Unlimited*, March 26, 2005.

"WMD Commission Stonewalls," *The Nation*, April 1, 2005.

"Bush asked to explain UK war memo," *CNN.com*, May 12, 2005.

"Memo: Bush manipulated Iraq intel," *Knight Ridder Newspaper*, May 9, 2005.

"The Secret Way to War," Mark Donner, *The New York Review of Books*, June 9, 2005.

Chapter Four

—————•◦•—————

RESULTING DECLINE IN U.S. FOREIGN POLICY AND NATIONAL SECURITY

Two needless right-wing wars damaged our foreign policy and led to losses of over four trillions of dollars and a decline in our national security. Other shortfalls were policies in combating international terrorism, controlling nuclear weapons and developing a missile shield.

An Unacceptable Foreign Policy

In campaigning for the first of the two terms of his presidency, President Bush took the view that America, then the only remaining superpower, should exercise restraint and project humility in our relations with other countries – "and this will be the spirit of my administration."

Instead, the spirit of his right-wing administration was just the opposite. He and his advisors took an arrogant, "my way or the highway" posture, acting unilaterally instead of working with the international community on common problems.

Anytime presidents make war-like gestures toward other countries with which they disagree, they encourage public support of bad regimes and make it nearly impossible for the world community to resolve tough problems diplomatically.

In 2004, a Defense Science Board study reported that there is worldwide anger and discontent over the ways the U.S. pursues its goals, and these ways have "... played straight into the hand of al-Qaeda." In 2005, a national news columnist spent ten days touring four European countries. He found universal dislike and distrust of the President.[1]

A letter to Secretary of State Powell explains why a high level diplomat, who had served in US embassies from Tel Aviv to Casablanca to Yerevan, resigned his position in the Bush administration. This letter is a wide-ranging and eloquent analysis of how the war in Iraq and our foreign policy has affected our position around the world (See Appendix I).

An Ineffective War Powers Act

The War Powers Act of 1973 sought to clarify under our Constitution the divided powers between Congress and the President to make war. It provides procedures for Congress to participate in decisions of the president to send our Armed Forces into hostilities.

The Act requires that the President report to Congress on use of U.S. Armed Forces and to end their use within 60 to 90 days unless Congress authorizes further action. The exception is an immediate need to repel an attack on the United States. The effectiveness of this Act and its constitutionality has been questioned ever since it was first enacted. [2]

Under a right-wing presidency our military forces, National Guard and Reserves were tied up on two costly and almost never ending wars. Chapter three describes how these two wars could have been avoided if the administration had not already made up its mind, and instead gathered the facts and used common sense. Chapter seven describes how Congress and the media had a real opportunity to stop both wars, but didn't.

The Chairman of the Joint Chiefs, in a special message to Congress in 2006 admitted that the two wars would make it far more difficult to respond to "future acts of aggression ... or to prevent a conflict in another part of the world." [3]

Meanwhile, tens of thousands of veterans have gone through hell with record suicides, posttraumatic stress disorder, drug addiction, unemployment and homelessness. Thousands others live without limbs or suffer brain trauma and other horrific wounds.

Two analysts – a former official of the Commerce Department and a former Chairman of the Council of Economic advisors – teamed up to estimate the full cost of the war in Iraq. Based on the upfront costs and long-term costs that stretch over decades they conservatively estimated it to be at least $3 trillion. The long-term costs include such things as disability of returning veterans, equipment replacement and increased borrowing to fund the war. [4]

The Eisenhower Research Project at Brown University completed, in 2011, a "Costs of War" analysis of **both** wars over the past decade. Some of its findings were:

- Combined deaths in and out of uniform – 225,000.
- Injury and illness of U.S. military – 550, 000.
- Costs ranging from $3.2 to $4 trillion.
- People displaced – 7,800,000.
- Democracies in Iraq and Afghanistan continue to rank low in political freedom. (http://costsofwar.org)

The trillions of dollars spent on these wars are not now available to invest in U.S job creation, education, modernizing our infrastructure, new energy technologies or stabilizing Medicare and Social Security programs. There is no evidence that the vast expenditures on two right-wing wars made us more secure.

As the wars dragged on, their proponents in Congress and the administration seemed increasingly indifferent to the suffering and loss of life of others while they, themselves, were out of harm's way. Eisenhower and Kennedy served in combat and, as President, they made every attempt to avoid going to war. Presidents who followed neither served in war nor used it as a absolute last resort.

It is too easy today to start wars and terribly difficult to end them. It's easy to start wars when less than one percent of the population participates and future generations have to pay the bill. The all-volunteer military of today is removed from society in general and is not representative of the population as a whole.

As Richard Cohen of the *Washington Post* pointed out, "This is a military conscripted by culture and class-induced ... (and) honored by those of us who would not, for a moment, think of doing the same". He goes on to say:

> *"Had there been a draft, the war in Iraq might never have been fought – or would have produced the civil protests of the Vietnam War era. The Iraq debacle was made possible by a professional military and by going into debt. George W. Bush didn't need your body or ... or your money. Southerners would fight and foreigners would buy the bonds".* [5]

In blunt statements to West Point Cadets in 2011, Defense Secretary Gates said that:

- **It would be unwise for us to ever fight another war, like Iraq or Afghanistan, and that the chances of carrying out a change in foreign government in that fashion were slim.**

- **Any future defense secretary who advises the president to again send a big American land army into Asia or into the Middle East or Africa ought to have his head examined.**

- **As the prospects for another head-on clash of large mechanized land armies seem less likely, the Army will be increasing challenged to justify the size, and costs of its heavy formations.**

- **The Army and the rest of the government must focus on capabilities that can prevent festering problems from growing into full-blown crises which require costly – and controversial – large-scale American military intervention.** [6]

A more disciplined use of the War Powers Act is required because (1) a president, even a well-intentioned one, can find a rationale for using our overwhelming military power and (2) there is a likelihood of finding military support for such a war in order to test advanced-technology weapons in a real world environment.

We can be a model for other countries, and we can advise and assist them. We cannot forcibly remake other countries in our image without losing our own identity. A further discussion of U.S. presidents promoting democracy around the world can be found in the previous chapter. The War Powers Act must be amended to prevent future Presidents from going on military adventures.

Forging a New Terrorism Policy

Following 9/11, Al-Qaeda had grown world-wide and established a foothold in Muslim countries in the Middle East, central Asia and North Africa. Their ranks have swollen and they have fomented attacks around the world.

After a year at war in Iraq and stalling for several months, the Bush right-wing administration finally released a report showing a massive increase in world-wide terrorism for 2004 – triple that of the previous year. Even greater increases were reported for 2005.

An Asia-Pacific conference on security concluded that the world was losing the war on terror because the United States had expanded the sea of hatred and deep-seated rage in the Muslim world. The use of military force, they said, would not solve this problem.

British intelligence reports that their support of the war in Iraq led to an upsurge in terrorist recruitment and at least thirty plots to kill people and damage the British economy. According to 100 American leading foreign policy analysts, we were failing to make progress in the global war on terror and the world has grown more, not less, dangerous.

Wars are not the answer to organized mobile terrorist networks. As these wars dragged on, they served as a powerful tool for recruiting new terrorists. Muslims from as far as a thousand miles away joined in a holy war against us and our allies.

Terror networks are often international activities that move from country to country. They must be dismantled with specially trained Elite Forces, using good intelligence, and international cooperation. There must be a global crackdown on sources of terror funds and far less U.S. dependence on Mideast oil.

All nations should address root causes of terrorist activities, dismantle them in their own countries, carefully secure nuclear material and help others do the same. A comprehensive policy along these lines for consideration follows.

- **Establish an international agreement of no sanctuary for countries harboring terrorist networks whose purpose it is to undermine other governments and harm innocent citizens. Any country that fails to cooperate in a serious way to remove such networks would automatically lose its right of sovereignty and be subject to international intervention. This is based on the right of self-defense.**

- **Use diplomacy, good intelligence, international cooperation, and mobile Elite Special Forces to find and take down terrorist command structures and training camps wherever they may be.**

- **Outlaw bomb-making nuclear material, inspect all countries that might give such material to terrorists, and enforce severe penalties for violations.**

- **Withdraw from foreign lands military occupational forces that are, as U.S. Senatorial candidate Tim Kaine said, "more positioned to fight past wars than to handle security challenges of today and tomorrow".**

- **Focus on root causes of international terrorist activities and use strong international pressure to help Israel and Palestine find a bold and imaginative solution to their 60 year-old conflict.**

- **Encourage religious spokespeople to stress the many similarities between Christian, Jewish and Muslim faiths.**

- **Hold periodic meetings among Heads of State on global terrorism to review progress, hold each other accountable and find solutions for the conduct of outlaw nations.**

- **Establish a high national security goal of energy independence in order to curb our dangerous reliance on oil producing countries, help protect the global oil supply, support a growing new energy economy and reduce the funds available to finance terrorists.**

This terrorism policy would be much more effective than wars and provides a sounder financial footing for our country to do what must be done with our dwindling resources. A key part of the policy is to clearly establish that any nation, which harbors international terrorists that rain death and destruction on other countries, has automatically lost its rights of sovereignty.

A country in danger of losing its sovereignty would have one of three options (1) remove the terrorist group within a certain timeframe, or (2) do so with the help of other countries, or (3) have their terrorist groups removed unilaterally by an international coalition.

Had it not been for the heroic action at 9/11 by passengers of the seized commercial aircraft over Pittsburgh, either the U.S. Congress or the White House would have been obliterated and our government disabled. It's time to really get serious.

At Heads of State Summits and UN meetings, countries harboring terrorist must be put on notice that they will be reckoned with and severely punished by the international community. People everywhere need to hope that one day the threat of terrorism will fade away and we can return to more peaceful ways—without a fortress mentality.

Nuclear Disarmament

Nuclear proliferation is the preeminent national security issue of our time. Under the Nuclear Nonproliferation Treaty, countries with nuclear arms are committed to negotiating disarmament. The purpose of this treaty is to, one day, permit freedom from the fear of nuclear extermination. However, many non-nuclear states are not satisfied with the progress to date of the larger powers, and some like North Korea and Iran, are trying to join the nuclear club.

Over the years a number of countries have joined this nuclear club, once monopolized by the U.S and Russia. Under a 1970's worldwide nonproliferation treaty, nations without nuclear weapons pledge not to pursue them, in exchange for a commitment by nuclear states to negotiate toward disarmament. However, many countries believe the nuclear states are moving too slowly.

In particular, they were concerned with the Bush right-wing administration decisions to reject a nuclear test ban, build new nuclear weapons, and devaluate treaties and the authority of international law.

A 2005 worldwide U.N. conference held in the U.S. was supposed to close gaping holes in the nuclear treaty. Neither President Bush nor his Secretary of State found time to attend that conference, and it failed. Afterwards, former Secretary of Defense Robert McNamara wrote an article stating that the world can no longer tolerate nuclear weapons and urged the U.S. to lead the way toward their elimination.[7]

Since the failed U.N. conference, a dozen countries have looked into this issue and, in June 2006, reported the following:

- **A serious and dangerous loss of momentum has occurred and nuclear states no longer take their commitment to disarmament seriously.**

- **Nuclear weapons number 27,000 worldwide. The count will rise because of efforts to develop more sophisticated new weapons and *place them in space*.**

- **Nuclear weapons should all be banned as unlawful, as is the case with biological and chemical weapons, and their use made unthinkable.**

- **A planned U.S. missile shield will lead to countermeasures by Russia and China.**

- **The U.S. has not ratified the Comprehensive Test Ban Treaty and its unwillingness to cooperate in international arms agreements is undermining efforts to curb nuclear weapons.**

- **If the U.S. takes the lead, the world will follow; if not, there will be more nuclear tests and new nuclear arms races will ensue.**

Instead of taking the lead on disarmament, the Bush right-wing administration put a new nuclear weapon in the works – a hydrogen bomb. Afterwards, in January 2007, atomic scientists moved the doomsday clock to five minutes before midnight.

A prestigious scientific committee that included two former secretaries of state (Henry Kissinger and George Schultz), two former secretaries of defense (Robert McNamara and William Perry), and former Armed Services Committee Chairman Sam Nunn called for the U.S. to take the lead in reversing reliance on nuclear weapons and in taking these weapons off standby alert.

It is impossible to imagine the utter destruction that can result from one of today's nuclear bombs – even a small one. Robert McNamara characterized our nuclear policy and its "hair-trigger" response as immoral, illegal, militarily unnecessary, and dreadfully dangerous. He stated his belief that the U.S. must lead the way toward elimination of these weapons around the world and should no longer rely on them as a foreign policy tool.[8]

Former Soviet President Mikhail Gorbachev commented favorably on the 2010 Senate ratification of the U.S. - Russia nuclear arms treaty. He said that what remains to be done is to ratify the treaty banning nuclear testing. The stalemate on that agreement has lasted for more than a decade. In order for it to go into effect, all forty-four nuclear technology states must sign and ratify it.

Nine, including the U.S., have not. A verifiable system is nearly in place and Gorbachev believes that, if the U.S. agrees to the test ban, most of the remaining countries will follow.[9] The UN Secretary has urged these nine countries to please ratify the treaty.

Progress is being made in the international community on securing materials used for nuclear weaponry and keeping them out of the hands of would be terrorists. The Obama administration held a second summit among nations on this issue in March 2012.

The Missile Shield

Shortly after the Bush right-wing administration took office, it withdrew from the Antiballistic Missile Treaty and restarted the very expensive Reagan "Star Wars" program. That system's "kill vehicles" are intended to fly into space and destroy enemy warheads. The new missile shield was initially supposed to be deployed by 2004. Hurried development led to incomplete testing and technical glitches.[10]

A more limited version has been under development ever since and subjected to carefully scripted tests. The limited version cannot cope with sizeable nuclear arsenals or clouds of decoys that might confuse it. In a late 2010 test the missile was unable to intercept a ballistic missile target.[11]

It is nearly impossible to hit a bullet with a far-a-away bullet, especially one that has countermeasures, like decoys. No real-world testing of the missile shield has yet proven successful.

A missile shield designed for ballistic missiles is of no use during a terrorist attack. Our coastal cities are vulnerable to missile or rocket attacks fired by terrorists off the U.S. coast. A renowned journalist questions whether preoccupation with the enormously expensive missile shield has short changed our defense against the more likely threat of shorter range terrorist's attacks from our east or west coast? [12]

Weapons in Space

For several decades, a worldwide treaty universally banned weapons in space. However, the Bush right-wing administration also withdrew the U.S. from that treaty and directed that new space weapons be developed. These weapons have enormous implications for our deficit-ridden budgets and relationships with other countries. Like airways, no one owns space. Other countries, fearing these new weapons, may be forced to join us in the race for space weaponry.

In 2008, Russia and China proposed a Space Arms Treaty but the U.S. refused to participate. China has since been active in this field and a new arms race could ensue. Neither China nor the U.S. has been eager to share technology. There's been little reporting on weaponization of space in recent times except to say that the U.S. and China Presidents pledged in a 2011 meeting to continue cooperative efforts.[13]

Conclusions and Remedies

The Congress needs to take another look at how the authority to declare war is being exercised under our Constitution. In addition to a debate on alternatives to war outlined in chapter three, Congress needs to budget responsibly for wars and arrange for fuller participation across our society in the hostilities that follow. In World War II, President Franklin Roosevelt had three sons in the military and one hit Normandy Beach in France.

As many Americans as possible should feel they have a stake in the war. The critical factors are shared sacrifice and pay as you go for any extended war. Congress should require that:

- Any future war be accompanied by increased tax revenues to pay for it and a temporary re-institution of the draft to provide the necessary manpower.
- Able-bodied persons not be exempted from war, including the rich, the famous, the powerful and especially those who hyped and voted for it. All, not just a small segment, should share in the burden of war.
- Responses to terror attacks from networks being harbored by other countries be carried out under a new comprehensive policy that involves participation of the international community and use of elite Special Forces with maximum mobility rather than wars.

Over decades, many countries have become concerned over the slow progress of the larger powers in responding to the nuclear disarmament treaty. Some have since joined the nuclear club, while others remain frustrated.

Previous right-wing administrations did not take a leadership role in outlawing the nuclear weapons and now two recalcitrant regimes, neither a free democracy, are threatening to add their names to the growing nuclear club.

The issue is how does the deterrence value of nuclear weapons fit in today's world? If such weapons did not exist, America would still remain the most powerful nation and be able to defend itself. The U.S. should seriously reexamine the value of nuclear weapons and work with the international community on a treaty to dismantle them worldwide as unthinkable weapons.

———

ENDNOTES

1. "Bush silence would speak to Europe," Tom Friedman, *New York Times*, Feb. 1, 2005.
2. *War Powers Act*, Public Law 93-148, 93rd Congress, H.J.Res. 542, November 7, 1973. CRS Report for Congress on The War Powers Resolution, Richard Grimmett, March 11, 2004.
3. "Wars put U.S. forces at risk abroad, Myers says," *Los Angeles Times*, May 3, 2005.
4. "The Iraq War Will Cost us $3 Trillion, and Much More," Linda Bilmes and Joseph Stiglitz, *Washington Post*, March 9, 2008.
5. "How little the U.S. knows of war," Richard Cohen, *Washington Post*, Jan. 4, 2011.
6. "Gates Warns Against More Wars Like Iraq and Afghanistan," Thom Shanker, *Truthout*, Feb. 25, 2011.
7. "Apocalypse Soon," Robert McNamara, *Foreign Policy*, May/June 2005.
8. Ibid
9. "The Senate's Next Task: Ratifying the Nuclear Test Ban Treaty," Mikhail Gorbachev, *New York Times*, Dec. 28, 2010.
10. "U.S. Missile Defense Test Again Fails Key Test," Ann Tyson, *Washington Post*, Feb. 15, 2005
11. "Long-range missile defense test fails," *CNN U.S.*, Dec. 2010.
12. "The Real Missile Defense Gap," David Ignatius, *Washington Post*, Mar. 23, 2005.
13. "Slow progress in U.S.-China space efforts," *spacedaily.com*, Jan. 22, 2011.

Chapter Five

PASSING ON A NATION IN DECLINE

During the first two presidential terms of this century, right wing administrations were fiscally irresponsible while at the same time ignoring glaring domestic needs on which our nation's future depends. What would conditions be like if they regain power for yet another term? This chapter and the next one will give you some idea.

Fiscal Irresponsibility

Our long-term fiscal health is being jeopardized by huge deficits, a staggering national debt, and *annual* interest approaching nearly a half trillion dollars a year.[1]

At the beginning of this century, a right-wing administration inherited a growing economy, a balanced budget and large surpluses. After two terms, it handed the next administration huge deficits and a failing economy that turned out to be much worse than anticipated.

Even before the disastrous economic downturn, analysts predicted that the next president would (1) be stuck with financial commitments that would rise dramatically in the year before he took office and (2) spend the entire four-year term "figuring out how to accommodate the long-range cost of Bush's policies."[2]

As noted in an Atlantic magazine article by James Fallows, the first action of the new administration had to be to contain the national emergency or accept the dire consequences of an unknown magnitude. He cites Senator Webb's advice from an economist before the historic vote: "you have to keep the financial system from going into cataclysmic default".

Going back to the 80's, Republicans had quadrupled the national debt during a 12 year period. Ross Perot's Independent Party then challenged Republicans for fiscal irresponsibility and they lost the '92 election to President Clinton. After Clinton balanced the budget and gave Republicans large surpluses, history did repeat itself and this time they managed to double the national debt during an eight year reign.

The Republican Party owns much of today's increasing federal debt because the millions of job losses and massive declines in tax revenues that occurred during presidential transition could not possibly be reversed in the near term. Federal tax collections were at their very lowest percentage of the economy in sixty years. And, deficits were structured long-term because of unwise tax cuts and difficult to end wars. [3]

Right-wing leaders in Congress voted seven times during the presidency of George W. Bush to raise the federal debt limit. For example, in May 2003 one of the debt limit increases passed the Senate the very same day as tax cuts for the wealthy. In total, right-wing big spenders (still in Congress) raised the debt limit by $4 trillion.[4] During that time their Vice-President said "deficits don't matter".

According to a *Washington Post* analysis of Congressional Budget Office 2011 data, right wing era policies account for more than $7 trillion of the increased federal debt and the Obama era policies account for about $1.7 trillion. The right-wing deficits were long-term and unnecessary; the Obama era ones were temporary and done to avert a national crisis.[5]

A substantial amount of our national debt is owned by foreign countries like China, Japan and Korea. A great deal of the interest income flows abroad, not here. Asian countries could one day hold us hostage. This untenable situation limits the flexibility of future presidents on foreign policy and in investing in our future.

Downturn in the Economy

The horrific economic conditions existing at the time of presidential transition are well known and further discussed in the next chapter. While our country was teetering on the edge of a second Great Depression, the right wing rejected government intervention with The American Recovery and Reinvestment Act on the grounds that the market would simply take care of things.

They consistently obstructed the new President's efforts at recovery and assistance to businesses who were bordering on bankruptcy. They wanted these businesses to live or die on their own. This approach was discredited during the Great Depression when there was no available credit; thousands of companies were going bankrupt; and unemployment rose to 25 percent. Many people committed suicide.

Former Secretary of Treasury Henry Paulsen (a Republican) estimated that there would be 25% unemployment again if the government had not swiftly intervened. Certainly, many more businesses would have suffered a severe setback or gone under through no fault of their own.

Without private capital, two major automobile companies would not have been given a second chance. The right wing characterizes the auto loans as bailouts. Actually they were loans and required the auto industry to (1) restructure their businesses and (2) repay the loans with interest. The absence of credit would have meant ceasing automobile production in 2009, causing reverberations throughout the entire auto sector and losses of jobs in the millions.[5a]

In 2012, GM announced its highest profit ever of 7.6 billion. Had the right wing had their way, GM and Chrysler and many of their suppliers across the country might have gone bankrupt and other countries handed a large share of **our** auto market.

The assistance provided to financial institutions and businesses did help reverse the economy's downward spiral. About two-thirds of the relief authorized by Congress was actually spent and all but about four percent of it is expected to be repaid.[6] Collapse of our financial institutions and liquidation of the auto industry would have moved the U.S. toward a second-rate power.

Now that the country is much better off than when the economy was in freefall, it is easy to challenge government intervention. The fact is anyone, who was in charge at the time, would have done everything humanely possible to avert another Great Depression—especially if they had lived through one or knew of the suffering it caused.

Ignoring Energy Independence

Our foreign policy has been enslaved by excessive reliance on Mideast oil. We own only two percent of the world's oil reserves but consume more than 20 percent. Continued refusal of right-wing leadership to break the stranglehold of foreign oil has endangered our national security and discouraged new energy business ventures.

The U.S. Council on Foreign Relations warned President Bush in 2001 that oil consumption was at an all-time high and that the energy sector was in a critical condition. They said our dependency made us vulnerable to oil-rich nations and limited our influence around the world. A crisis could erupt at any time.[7]

Other consuming giants, like China and India, are seriously competing with us for oil, and the surge in demand will surely one day outstrip world supply. These two energy consuming giants are seeking access to limited world resources and they will inevitably clash with the West.[8]

China anticipated this crisis and has become the world's largest maker of wind turbines and the world's largest manufacturer of solar panels. Although solar panel technology was invented here, the right-wing obsession with oil has allowed this country to fall behind and U.S. businesses now find it more difficult to compete.

According to a *Scientific American* analysis, our planet can be powered largely with renewable wind, water and solar energy if there is the political will and leadership. The change in energy use would be based largely on today's technologies and zero emissions of green house gases and air pollution.

This transition would create huge savings for our country because electrical energy is more efficient than gasoline energy. The sources of such energy would be beyond future human demand, ultimately be as cheap as coal, and have less downtime.

A new report in 2011 by a U.N. Intergovernmental Panel concluded that renewable energy is an increasingly practical and promising option. The fuel is free and operating costs are low. Costs are likely to decline as innovation accelerates and global energy demand continues to rise.

To illustrate its prospects, the global research director of GE has announced plans to open a solar panel manufacturing plant in 2013 that will create enough solar panels yearly to power about 80,000 homes.

The idea is to give the world "a new, efficient, energy system rather than the old, dirty, inefficient one." The obstacles are primarily political, not technical. Legislators crafting policy would have to find ways to resist lobbying by the entrenched oil energy industries. These industries are major contributors to the right-wing of the Republican Party. [9] The right wing is deeply invested in them and is actively hostile to energy alternatives.

To begin to close the gap between our consumption of 20 percent of the world's oil and our production of only 2 percent, the current administration has embarked on a decade-long strategy to develop all sources of American energy. It covers wind, solar, biofuels, increased production of oil and natural gas, and ways to reduce oil consumption. Unfortunately, that strategy is limited to executive action because the right-wing continues to forestall major progress in Congress.

According to Michael T. Klare, professor of world security studies at Hampshire University, how we characterize our energy predicament in the coming decades and which of two paths we select will in large measure determine the fate of our nation.

> *One path is to resemble a Third World petro-state, with compliant government leaders, increasingly money-ridden and corrupt political system, and negligible environmental and health safeguards. The other path is to pursue far greater investment in the development of renewable energies and remain a First World nation with strong health and environmental regulations and robust democratic institutions.*

A time and place in history awaits a President and Congress who together will (1) tell the American people the real price of our dependence on foreign oil (including wars), (2) call on our entrenched oil industries to diversify, and (3) establish a Manhattan-style project to (a) eliminate America's dependence on foreign oil, (b) build a clean energy economy and (c) save our ailing planet from climate change.

Refusal to Accept Growing Threat of Climate Change

Climate change is considered the greatest threat facing civilization—no less than our planet is at stake. The Antarctic ice shelf is collapsing and huge areas of frozen ground in Siberia and Alaska are thawing. Next will be droughts, flooding of major cities in low lying areas, wildfires and deaths of plants and animal species. Cold weather species, like polar bears, are already dwindling toward extinction. When the damage passes the tipping point and becomes irreversible, it will ruin life on earth for future generations.

In a 2007 bleak and powerful assessment of the future of the planet, a leading international network of scientists concluded that a massive effort is needed to slow down the pace of global climate disruption before intolerable consequences become inevitable.[10] In the global scientific community there is near unanimous agreement that climate change is real and that humans contribute to the pending catastrophe.

Global emissions of carbon dioxide increased by 45 % during the last two decades and reached an all-time high in 2010 of 33 billion tons. According to the Department of Energy, this increase is largely driven by three countries – USA, China and India.

The point of no return is perilously close, according to the former head of the U.N. He says climate change has profound implications for human well-being ranging from jobs and health, to food and security. The question, he says, is not whether climate change is happening but whether, in face of this emergency, we can change fast enough.

We are the largest producer of greenhouse gas emissions, yet we ranked fifty-three out of fifty-six countries in controlling them. These gases block the escape of heat from earth by acting as an insulating blanket. Countries in Europe are so concerned that they are imposing a tax on their emissions, called the carbon tax. The bottom line is that human habitation and the earth's survival is at stake.

The threat of climate change could disrupt all civilization as we know it and make our country unsafe for millions.[11] Postponing action will simply require more resources and time to combat the threat, if there still is enough time left. Whether the warnings are as bad as most scientists predict is *not* the real issue. Responsible action will lead to new energy industries, millions of new jobs, energy independence, and obviously make our planet a lot safer place to live.

A leading scientist at Massachusetts Institute of Technology (MIT), a Republican, has gradually realized the seriousness of climate change based on the accumulated evidence. He considers those who won't accept this evidence as radical, not conservative.[12] As one writer said, "the failure of the United States to get serious about climate change is unforgivable – a human folly beyond imagining."

A respected physicist at the University of California (Richard Muller) dismissed for years climate research as being "polluted by political and activist frenzy". But, after examining data five times greater than other researchers, he now says "global warming is real".

Pulitzer Prize winning journalist Eugene Robinson reported that Mr. Muller's findings have reduced many deniers to incoherent grumbling or stunned silence. Robinson concludes that "It is the know-nothing politicians – not scientists – who are committing fraud."

Once the adverse planetary affects take hold, we may or may not be able to save the world. Whether we do or not, the damage will be enormous. For example, what will happen to low lying coastal areas here and elsewhere when Antarctica, the massive continent at the southern tip of the world, begins to melt?

Gambling with the end of the world is not a sound way to keep a political party viable. If right-wing views remain unchanged, it could very well lead to the demise of their own party. They will need a new name, new philosophy, new leadership and new ways to replace lost supporters.

With climate change repeatedly stalled in Congress, a group of kids, led by a 17 year old, filed 10 lawsuits against the federal government and individual states to compel them to take action. These suits are based on the premise that governments hold natural resources in trust for their citizens and bear the fiduciary obligation to protect these resources for future generations.

The suits ask the federal government to prepare a national climate recovery plan that caps greenhouse gas emissions and reduces them by six percent each year. The kids believe that their generation and the next "are going to have to work hard to fix this mess." [12a]

Reinforcing these suits are three new reports in 2012, one from a non-profit group, Climate Central, and two others published in the peer-reviewed journal, Environmental Research Letters. They report that five million people, as well as businesses and infrastructure, residing in low-lying coastal areas in the United States are vulnerable to rising sea levels fueled by the melting of glaciers and ice sheets. South Florida, because of its geology and system of drainage, may become "indefensible".

Finally, a March, 2012 report of the World Meteorological Organization confirms that climate change is happening now. It concludes that accelerated climate change, driven by human activity, has led to soaring temperatures around the world and the decade between 2001 and 2010 was the warmest ever recorded in all continents of the globe.

"Many people today still assume – mistakenly – that the earth is so big that we human beings cannot possibly have any major impact on the way our planet's ecological system operates. That assertion may have been true at one time, but it's not the case anymore. We have grown so numerous and our technologies have become so powerful that we are now capable of having a significant influence on many parts of the Earth's environment. The most vulnerable part of the Earth's ecological system is the atmosphere. It's vulnerable because it's so thin."

AN INCONVIENT TRUTH
AL GORE

A Broken Health Care System Left Unattended

Health care is a basic human necessity. All of us and our families need health-care services at some point in our lives. The basic idea of reform is that everyone must pay something toward their own healthcare without being subjected to financial ruin. And, those who do pay should not be expected to assume responsibility for those who not do.

More than half of all Americans have no insurance or inferior coverage or unaffordable premium rates.[13] The U.S. is ranked 37th by the World Health Organization.

Reform is essential for saving lives, maintaining quality of life, and making health care affordable for the average American. In the '90's right-wing leadership opposed Clinton's health care reform for fear its popularity would cost them future elections. They have continued this obstruction in the current Congress and now have their sights set on repealing the new healthcare act.

They are not afraid that the reform will fail, but rather that it may succeed. Former Senate Republican Majority leader and top surgeon, Bill Frist, went public in 2011 to oppose his party's obstruction, urging them to improve the new ground-breaking legislation, not repeal it.

According to a 2012 Reuters/Ipsos poll, 65 percent of Americans favor parts of the current health care law and some believe that it should have gone further. However, our current system of relying on a for-profit privatized health insurance system is inherently inefficient and ineffective. To illustrate:

- Private insurers focus on those people unlikely to need much care because their incentives are to keep costs down and profits up.
- The collection of information by private insurers to drive away needy subscribers is costly and wasteful.
- Health care providers incur substantial billing and insurance costs for a variety of different insurance systems estimated at some $70,000 a year per physician.
- The privatized system discourages preventive health care.
- The privatized system drives the uninsured sick into expensive care settings, like hospitals and emergency rooms, and others have to bear the costs.
- Administrative costs, executive salaries and bonuses of private insurers far exceed that of a single-payer not-for-profit system.
- Other advanced countries with a single-payer system and universal coverage have a longer life expectancy and much lower costs than the U.S.[14]

The rising cost of private health insurance has imposed a heavy burden on most people. A potentially rewarding experiment would be to have competing alternatives, embodied in the current reform act, by adding a single payer system. It would give the American people a choice between private insurance companies and a single payer both as to benefits and costs.

The single-payer program eliminates the middle man (private insurer) who incurs administrative costs, executive salaries and bonuses, and profits – all of which feed on health care without materially improving it.

To illustrate the difference between the costs of privatized and a public single-payer systems, administrative costs for Medicare are 6 cents a dollar and for private insurers 25-30 cents a dollar. According to the Physicians for a National Health Program, One-third of the health care dollar goes not to them but to private insurance companies.

In 2011, Vermont was the first state to embark on a comprehensive single-payer system. It focuses on getting the right incentives embodied in our health care system. Minnesota and California are considering the system. A bipartisan Wyden-Brown amendment to current law would allow individual states to innovate on health care reforms.

As in other advanced countries, the single-payer alternative would drive down medical costs and insurance premiums while improving access to health care. A Rebuild the Dream Act introduced in Congress refers to this alternative as a public insurance option. Nurse Donna Smith, a cancer patient who may not survive publication of this book, said in a March 2012 article that a system is needed to:

"Advances human health care and doesn't drain personal wealth ... A single-payer model, with a progressively advanced financed, single standard of high quality is better for all of us—and I like a system that is better for all".

Having had experience with private insurance and a single payer system, the writer can unequivocally state that the doctor/patient relationship remains unchanged, as are the services received. There is no such thing as government-run top-down medical system except perhaps in the Veterans Administration.

Educational Decay

Our public school system has decayed and we are now running far behind other countries in such subjects as science and math. Working families are finding college costs increasingly unreachable for their children.

Education represents the long-term future of our country. Over the years, the right wing has tried to close down the Department of Education and is now attempting to defund its initiatives. When in charge its one effort, No Child Left Behind, has fallen short and led to mismanagement of our schools.[15]

The current administration is experimenting with incentives to improve our educational system. For example, the Department of Education (1) rewards school winners in a race to the top and (2) grants waivers to states from the No Child Left Behind law if they make acceptable reforms. Furthering these efforts is a popular NBC Education Nation program.

The eventual loss to our economy of a poorly educated populace is inestimable.

Misuse of Religion in Politics

Can religion play a role in government and politics without it being misused to trample the religious freedom of others? Our founding fathers were intent on keeping church and state firmly separated.

This constitutional separation has been eroded by recent right-wing administrations. One high official from the Bush administration said that the President "truly believes he's on a mission from God." Some of his followers are even convinced that he is a divinely chosen instrument of God."[16]

President Bush is reported to have said: "I trust God speaks through me." Right-wing Republican candidate Michele Bachmann said she had a "sense" from God to run for president in the upcoming 2012 election. Similar thoughts were expressed by presidential candidates Herman Cain and Governor Perry of Texas.

America was created with the freedom to worship any religion or to have no religion at all. An author on this subject has raised the question: are we a "society of inclusion, reason, diversity, or are we mandated to be a certain kind of intolerant Christian society?"[17] According to the great commentator, Walter Cronkite, the religious right has been, "... manipulating religion to further their intolerant political agenda."[18]

Episcopal minister and former Republican Senator John Danforth claimed in 2005 that his party's fixation on a religious agenda has turned it in the wrong direction. It is time, he says, for Republicans to rediscover their roots and worry about rising deficits.[19]

Any president's spiritual life is personal, and his work must stand or fall on its own merit. He should not suggest to the public that he knows God's will. President Lincoln had it right – don't try to prove God is on your side, prove instead that you are on God's side.

Rev. Dr. Graham Standish wrote a thought provoking article on today's political behavior and how it has been linked to the Christian religion. A Republican who voted for Reagan twice, Reverend Standish left his party to become an independent because of its "attack-and-accuse style" of politics and its "politics of self-interest" He says these tactics bring out the worst in human beings because the constant pursuit of power corrupts (See Appendix II).

Conclusions

The right-wing made virtually no progress on the domestic front during its two terms in office. It did attempt reforms on education and immigration, but failed on both. While it courageously addressed the difficult and complex issue of illegal immigration, an unworkable Congress was unable to resolve differences among its members and move forward.

The current administration has stepped up efforts to reduce illegal immigration and a further effort at a comprehensive solution may be in sight if Congress decides to become less partisan and reorganize how it operates (See chapter eight).

———

END NOTES

1. "Interest on the Debt Outstanding," *Treasury Direct*, Jan. 5 2011.
2. "After Bush Leaves Office, His Budget's Costs Balloon," Jonathan Weisman and Peter Baker, *Washington Post*, Feb. 14, 2005. "H.R. Perot, the U.S. needs you," Tom Blackburn, *The Palm Beach Post*, March 14, 2005. "Running in the Red: How the U.S., on the road to

surplus, detoured to massive debt," Lori Montgomery, *Washington Post*, April 30, 2011. "During the math on Obama's deficits", Ezra Klein, Wash. Post, Jan. 31, 2012.

3. "Second thoughts, Fed chief acknowledges 2001 tax cuts encouraged deficit," Neil Henderson, *Washington Post*, April 22, 2005.

4. "During Bush Presidency, Current GOP Leaders Voted 19 times To Increase Debt Limit By $4 Trillion", Travis Waldron, thinkprogress.org/politics, April 14, 2011.

5. "Running in the red: How the U.S., on the road to surplus, detoured to a massive debt," Lori Montgomery, *Washington Post*, April 30, 2011.

5a. "Delusions About the Detroit Bailout", Steven Rattner, *New York Times*, Feb. 23, 2012.

6. "Why Tarp has been a success story," Robert J. Samuelson, *Washington Post,* March 27, 2011.

7. "U.S. appears to have fought the war for oil and lost it." Ian Rutledge, *FT.com*, April 11, 2005. "Energy Insanity," Molly Ivins, *Working For Change,* March 29, 2005.

8. "The Axis of Oil," Jehangir Pocha, *In These Times*, Feb. 2, 2005.

9. "The Renewable Future," Yana, *Truthout,* May 15, 2011. "A Plan to Power 100 Percent of the Planet with Renewables," Mark Jacobson and Mark Delucchi, *Scientific American*, Oct. 26, 2009. "GE Sees Cheaper Than Fossil Power in Five Years," Brian Winefield, *Bloomberg*, May 26, 2011. "The Dirty Energy Party," *New York Times* Editorial, Feb. 21, 2011.

10. "Panel Issues Bleak Report on Climate Change," Elisabeth Rosenthal and Andrew C. Renkin, *New York Times*, Feb2, 2007.

11. "How we put the heat on nature," Robin McKie, *Guardian Unlimited*, Jan. 30, 2005.

12. "Scientist proves conservatism and belief in climate change aren't incompatible," Neela Banerjee, *latimes.com*, Jan. 5, 2011. "The scientific finding that settles the climate-change debate", Eugene Robinson, The Washington Post, October 24, 2011.

12a. "The young and the restless: Kids sue government over climate change", Claire Thompson, Grist, Dec. 8, 2011.

13. "Study: 20 Million U.S. Workers Lack Health Insurance," *Reuters*, April 27, 2005. "No insurance against going broke," Elizabeth Warren, *Washington Post*, Feb. 2005. "An Urgent Case For Fixing Health Care," David Broder, *Washington Post*, May 29, 2005.

14. "Universal Health Care: Can We Afford Anything Less?" Gerald Friedman, truthout.org, July 5, 2011.

15. "Report: NO Child Law Amiss," *New York Times*, Feb. 24, 2005. "Lawsuit Targets No Child Left Behind," *New York Times*, April 21, 2005. "Squandering America's Future," Robert Borosage, *Tom Paine Common Sense*, Feb. 8, 2005.

16. "What makes Bush's presidency so radical," Ron Suskind, *New York Times Magazine*, Oct. 17, 2004.

17. Freethinkers: A History of American Secularism, Owl Books, 2nd Reprint Edition, Jan. 7, 2005.

18. An undated Dear Friend Letter from the Desk of Walter Cronkite.

19. "In the Name of Politics," John Danforth, *New York Times*, March 30, 2005. "Moderate Christians' alternate vision," John Danforth, *New York Times*, June 19, 2005.

CHAPTER SIX

A SECOND REJECTION OF PEOPLE'S CHOICE OF PRESIDENT

The two-term right-wing administration left the most difficult set of challenges ever faced by a new president. They left him in an untenable position with a doubling of our national debt, two never ending wars and a failing economy. Banks were in crisis, credit markets were frozen. We were losing 800,000 jobs a month and Americans had lost $10 trillion in the stock market. Making recovery almost insurmountable was a deeply partisan system of doing business in Congress.

From the very outset, right-wing leaders opposed the new President, Barack Obama, every step of the way. According to them, the President has done nothing right since coming to office. If they saw any kind of a victory for the President, they misrepresented it and blocked it. When they presented alternatives to the President's proposals, they were mainly worn out ideas from their previous agenda that had failed our country in the past and contributed to the mess we're in today.

Ruthless Obstruction Returns Big Time

Right–wing leaders made a strategic decision not to work with the President and instead forced his party to govern alone. They spent their efforts almost entirely on obstructing recovery rather than on developing their own ideas and capacity to govern under very difficult circumstances. As a consequence, the public got the benefit of only a partial governing body in Congress with the minority constantly obstructing the majority.

Their alternatives presented to the President's proposals were the trickle-down tax cuts that had failed our country in the past decade and a market approach that had no relevance to a national economy in crisis.

Right wing leaders obstructed passage of several Jobs and unemployment bills. These bills were necessary to maintain the lifeline of struggling Americans and small businesses. Americans who required this assistance had nothing to do with the economic crisis. The right-wing leaders, who refused this assistance, did.

To regain power in the 2012 elections, the right wing is now relying on a recession weary electorate – a recession created during its time in office. They are also relying on a narrative which is at odds with the facts and rational thinking. It takes the form of fear, deception, and hate-inspiring rhetoric. It turns people against people and party against party.

This narrative deceives the public about who President Obama is and what his intentions are. The right wing gives credence to wild assertions about his birthplace, religion and political leanings. Their idea is – he is not like us, he's un-American.

At town hall meetings right-wing supporters packed pistols, displayed despicable signs and shouted down others. They demonized opponents and used fear-mongering and intimidation tactics. Although the right-wing position is that both sides do this sort of thing, the *New Yorker* magazine strongly disagreed:

> **"Only one side has made the rhetoric of armed revolt against an oppressive tyranny the guiding spirit of its grassroots movement and its midterm campaign. Only one side routinely invokes the Second Amendment as a form of swagger and intimidation... Only one side's activists bring guns to Democratic political gatherings. Only one side has a popular national TV host who uses his platform to indoctrinate viewers in the conviction that the President is an alien, totalitarian menace to the country. Only one side fills the AM waves with rage and incendiary falsehoods. Only one side has an iconic leader, with**

a devoted grassroots following, who can't stop using violent imagery and dividing her countrymen into us and them, real and fake." [1]

A Homeland Security Agency report warned that right-wing extremism was on the rise with growing potential for violence. Some right wing extremists have also threatened to use guns as a political solution. [2] Violence has erupted at congressional offices, and congressional members and the President has received numerous death threats.

Rather than toning down the rhetoric of their supporters, right wing leaders in Congress and elsewhere pander to them. And, they set poor examples by being disrespectful to their colleagues and the President. As just one illustration, in 2012, Republican House member Fitzpatrick of Pennsylvania referred to the President as treasonous.

The problem is that thoughtful voices of moderate conservatives in the business and religious communities and elsewhere have been drowned out. Research at the University of Michigan reveals the dangers of a right-wing messaging machine drumming the wrong kind of information into minds of the less informed. The research found that:

- When misinformed political partisans are exposed to corrected facts in news stories they rarely changed their minds.
- We often base our opinions on our beliefs – and, rather than facts driving beliefs, our beliefs can dictate the facts we choose to accept. They can cause us to twist facts so they fit better with our preconceived notions. [3]

Right-wing leaders know, of course, that the crazy things being said about the President are untrue. They choose not to tell their supporters to be more civil. If they do, they may lose their support, and possibly their own jobs and an opportunity to return power.

At the end of the President's second year, more than half of his judicial nominees and many executive positions were still in limbo because right-wing members had blocked up or down votes. A federal court in Illinois had only one judge doing the jobs of four. The average civil litigant nationwide must wait two years for a jury trial. Nearly half of federal judgeships will be vacant by the end of the decade if the current confirmation rate does not speed up according to the Department of Justice's Office of Legal Policy.[4]

Right-Wing Holdover Leaders in Congress Thwart Progress

Senate and House leaders, Mitch McConnell and John Boehner, are holdovers from the past. They were key players during the two failed right-wing administrations. Since then their main accomplishments have been to obstruct, delay and block the new administration's initiatives. They set a record for use of the mere threat of a filibuster to block legislation. Filibusters increased from an average of twenty during a Congressional session to 136 in the last one. That easy weapon should never be in the hands of a power-obsessed minority.

When asked on *Meet the Press* in late 2010, Senate Republican Minority leader McConnell could not produce a single idea on how to cut deficits. He would make tax cuts for the rich permanent despite looming deficits. He acknowledged that reductions in spending would be forthcoming from the President's new Deficit (Bowles/Simpson) Commission.

What he neglected to say was that he and his fellow Republicans had already blocked a much stronger legislative version of that same Commission as soon as they discovered the President supported it. To deny the President a victory, several Republican co-sponsors voted to block their own resolution.

Later, right-wing leaders would not support recommendations of President's deficit-reducing Commission although some were highly regarded by members of both parties.

In a major speech on the economy in late 2010, Republican Minority leader Boehner lectured the audience on what he was against, but not on what he was for – except, of course, making tax cuts for the rich permanent. He offered no proposals, no plans and no agenda. Just before midterm elections, House leadership did unveil an agenda called a Pledge to America. It was strong on rhetoric and weak on action.

The Pledge would roll back regulations on Wall Street and banks and return to the Bush tax cuts and his spending levels. It ignored entitlement spending, a major part of our federal budget. It did nothing about our huge cold war defense budgets.[5] After opposing for months the President's tax cuts for small business, the Republican Pledge proposed one of its own.

In 2011, one right-wing Senator did his best to postpone a nuclear arms treaty with Russia that already had been exhaustively considered in congressional hearings and supported by leaders of both parties. Another right wing leader, put in charge of the House committee on government oversight, threatened non-stop investigations of the administration. And, still another, who represents big oil and now chairs the energy committee, declared war on the administration's energy policies that are trying to move us into the 21st century. (See chapter 5)

Slowing Down Economic Recovery to Regain Office

During transition, the President was faced with a near financial collapse similar to the one we experienced in the 1930's. Anyone who lived through that economic crash knows of its horrors and the seemingly endless recovery time.

The new President quickly intervened to stimulate the economy, save financial institutions and give our automobile industry a chance to recover. He also restored credit and assisted the housing industry. The alternative was an economic meltdown.

In referring to the horrendous situation that the President inherited, the Federal Reserve Chairman Ben Bernanke said the world was spared an even worse cataclysm that could have rivaled or surpassed the Great Depression. He and former Treasurer Secretary Paulsen, a Republican, believe that unemployment would have otherwise gone up as high as twenty-five percent.[6]

After regaining control of the House in 2011, right-wing leaders in Congress directed the nation's attention to deficits and women's rights and away from jobs and the economy. According to Senator Schumer, several legislative job creating initiatives, which the right-wing would normally support, were being blocked. He says Republicans are relying on the historical fact that no president suffering from high unemployment can be reelected.[7]

The President apparently has listened to President Truman's advisor in a similar situation. The advisor wrote Truman that the new Congress has:

"... agreed generally that cooperation is necessary. But, they have made it equally plain that their definition of cooperation is abdication by the executive... They believe their party has been given a mandate; that it is up to them and not the executive to set policy... The opposition believes also that they can elect their own president two years from now. But the best way to do it is by (showing) the people every day the presumed incompetence of the present administration." [8]

What If the Failing Right-Wing Agenda Returns?

If right-wing obstruction continues, America's progress will be slow during President Obama's remaining time in office. If *recent history* is any guide, here is what you can expect if the right wing of the Republican Party retakes control of government in 2012 or 2016:

- Big business, the wealthy and their lobbyists will heavily influence executive and legislative outcomes and income inequality will increase (see chapter seven).
- Our fiscal condition again will be in jeopardy due to unaffordable tax breaks for the wealthy and deregulation of financial institutions.
- Much of our debt will continue to be sold to Far East countries and they will have an ever increasing leverage over our foreign policy and domestic economy.
- Unemployment will increase because government will no longer invest in new technology and infrastructure and because trickle-down economics doesn't work, as proven by the right wing's negative job record during its last eight years in office.
- The Supreme Court will have a decided right-wing majority that will allow corporate and big money interests to continue to buy elections (See chapter seven).
- Emphasis will continue shifting from developing and producing American made products to further outsourcing of jobs overseas.
- Energy independence will continue to be ignored and our dangerous addiction to oil and coal pollutants will continue to dominate our energy policy with annual $4 billion unneeded subsidies to giant oil companies.

- Worldwide scientific evidence of climate change will continue to be rejected, even though responding to it is a win-win situation for America:
  - If the overwhelming evidence of climate change is wrong, a U.S. response will, nevertheless, create alternative sources of energy, more jobs, energy independence and a more livable planet.
  - If the overwhelming evidence is right, a U.S. response will help avoid a burnt-out planet, weather catastrophes, floods from melting glaciers and wars between countries over shortages of oil, food and water.
- We will return to ineffective, but expensive wars instead of relying on diplomacy, international cooperation and a new policy for coping with global terrorism (See chapter four).
- There will be a return to a diminished world view of America (See chapter four).
- We will not tightly control nuclear weapons or their testing or accelerate their dismantling (see chapter four).
- Our educational system will continue to decay, and there will be less financial aid for deserving people to earn college or other degrees and less effort to reduce unaffordable college tuition costs.
- Social Security, Medicare and Medicaid will not be modified to assure a safety net for future generations, but rather drastically reversed. Much of the population will have to cope with inadequate or no health care coverage and unaffordable costs.

Further Dangers of Reversing the Nation's Course

The American public is in the horns of a dilemma. It's only natural in tough times that people who are hurting economically will want to throw the incumbents out of office. On the other hand, returning the levers of power back to those who caused the tough times is only asking for trouble.

A Wall Street Journal report shows that during the right wing's eight years in power, it had the worst track record of job creation since the government began keeping records during President Truman's years.[9] Job losses accelerated to a high of 800,000 a month. From transition through the first two months of the Obama administration another two million jobs were lost.

Another reason for caution is the right wing's war-like mentality toward other nations, as described in Chapter 3. The right wing has yet to adopt tough diplomacy and international cooperation to resolve foreign policy problems.

If the right wing returns to power, its tendency will be to eradicate the progress made by the Obama administration. That is exactly what happened after its eight-year war with the two Clinton administrations. (See chapters two through five).

Recovering from a national crisis is not the right time to revert back to the political party that created it. Recovery must make the country stronger than it was before the economic collapse. The right wing has no realistic plan to achieve that extraordinarily difficult goal.

The right wing lacks the required diversity and capacity to govern because it has driven moderates out of the Republican Party. Without moderates, the right wing is unable to reach agreement with the other party on matters vital to the American people (See chapter eight).

Before being returned to power, the Republican Party must assume responsibility for today's conditions and replace their leaders with those who have the capacity to govern. They should select bold, broadminded, imaginative leaders who put their country first over party.

A Divided Country or Not

A national columnist wrote in 2011: "one of our two great political parties has made it clear that it has no interest in making America governable, unless it's doing the governing." President Obama's view is that "neither party, by itself, can realistically hope to solve the challenges faced by the United States."

"We will move ahead together, or not at all – for all the challenges we face are bigger than party, and bigger than politics. At stake right now is not who wins the next election ... At stake is whether new jobs and industries take root in this country or somewhere else. It's whether the hard work and industry of our people is rewarded. It's whether we

sustain the leadership that has made America not just a place on the map, but a light to the world."

State of the Union, 2011

President Lincoln's view is that "a divided country cannot long endure." Our Pledge of Allegiance says we are "one nation, indivisible". Over the next few years we will discover whether this is true. We have a choice; operate either as one country or two – one against the other.

––––––

END NOTES

1. "Arguing Tucson," George Packer, *The New Yorker*, Jan. 10, 2011. "Climate of Hate," Paul Krugman, *New York Times*, Jan 9, 2011.
2. "Rightwing Extremism: Current Economic and Political Climate Fueling Resurgence in Radicalization and Recruitment", U.S. Department of Homeland Security, April, 2009. "Climate of Hate," Paul Krugman, *New York Times*, Jan. 9, 2011.
3. "Facts Still Matter," Bill Moyers, *Truthout*, Feb. 14 2011.
4. "Think Progress", Jan. 23, 2011.
5. "An Alliance of opposites takes on Pentagon," Farah Stockman, *Boston Globe*, Nov. 21, 2010. "The Sustainable Defense Task Force Cuts," Mike Burleson, *New Wars*, June 21, 2010.
6. "Bernanke says policymakers prevented cataclysm worse than Great Depression," Neil Irwin, *Washington Post*, April 9, 2010. "Financial Meltdown Was Avoidable, Inquiry Concludes," Sewell Chan, *New York Times*, Jan. 25, 2011.
7. "Dems dig in: GOP trying to sabotage economy on purpose, Greg Sargent, Wash. Post, July 1, 2011.
8. "For Obama: Look to the public, not Congress," Dan Balz, *Washington Post*, Jan. 8, 2011.
9. "Bush On Jobs: The Worst Track Record On Record, The Wall Street Journal, January 9, 2009.

Chapter Seven

REPAIRING OUR SYSTEM OF DEMOCRACY

The Economist Intelligence Unit Index of Democracy rates all countries in sixty factors divided over five general categories: free and fair election process, civil liberties, functioning of government, political participation and political culture. The U.S. ranked 19th of world's 25 most advanced democracies.

The right wing likes to talk about America's exceptionalism. While we have been truly exceptional all during the last century, in recent times things have changed.

Of the world's most advanced democracies, the U.S. is ranked among the worst in categories of income inequality, student performance, unemployment, food insecurity, infrastructure, life expectancy, health care, and prison population. The 2011 Democracy report observes that:

"U.S. democracy has been adversely affected by a deepening of the polarization of the political scene and political brinkmanship and paralysis."

The International Monetary Fund forecasts that China's economy will surpass that of America's in just five years. Our next President may be the last one to preside over the world's largest economy.[1]

Institutions crucial to our democracy are failing us; Congress, an integral part of our system of checks and balances; the press/media, our watchdog over the three branches of government; and the Supreme Court, our savior of last resort. Putting our democracy in further disrepair are (1) an electoral system that works for political parties and big money interests, not for the American people and (2) an increasing income inequality among citizens. These matters are the subject of this and concluding chapter eight.

Congress and the Media Did Not Get the Job Done

Congress and the media should be asking tough questions and keeping the public well informed. During the last two decades, some members of Congress and the media were asleep at the switch while others sought power for themselves or became agents of the Executive Branch. Both institutions failed when the public needed them most.

During the Clinton two-term presidency the media did not expose the lengthy right-wing conspiracy or the conspirators themselves until several books finally set the record straight. The conspirators had only one thing in mind, force the President to resign and retake the executive powers they believed belonged to them (See chapter one).

With disclosure of the ongoing conspiracy, the presidential election that followed (the closest in history) would clearly have had a different outcome. And, the U.S. Supreme Court would not have had the opportunity In that presidential election to interfere with Florida's right to have its votes counted—as it actually did.

We would have continued on with the previous administration's priorities of balancing the federal budget with surpluses and directly confronting the immediate threat of further al-Qaeda's terrorist attacks on the United States (See chapter 2).

In a representative democracy, public opinion influences public policy and presidential elections. Success depends on whether Congress and the media keep the public well informed. When the Bush administration went astray, the public was not sufficiently informed of its performance until it was too late for the public to reject a second term and change the course of events.

A USA/Gallup poll rated President Bush's performance worse than any of his five predecessors. His performance also trailed recent presidents rejected for a second term. Yet, we reelected him.

The media and Congress never did seriously inquire into why President Bush obstructed the 9/11 investigation or why he resisted its creation in the first place. They did not delve deeply into *why* the roles of the President, the Vice-President and their national security team were conspicuously missing from the 9/11 Commission report.

Disclosure of their gross dereliction of duty leading up to 9/11 would surely have made President Bush unelectable for a second term. We would have had a different president in office, an earlier end to the war in Iraq, a different response to the Katrina disaster, and a national debt at least under some semblance of control.

There would have been no Supreme Court decision that now permits corporations to buy elections. That is because the two right-wing Justices who ruled in favor of that decision (Chief Justice Roberts and Justice Alito) would not have been on the bench had President Bush been limited to one term, as he should have been.

As to the Iraqi war, members of Congress did not ask the tough questions or examine U.S. intelligence in depth. Agency *dissents* and CIA *caveats* about the intelligence were not explored, nor were impartial or expert witnesses called. The Director for intelligence of the Joint Chiefs of Staff could have disclosed the great uncertainties and lack of evidence on Iraq's Weapons of Mass Destruction, but he was not called upon to testify.[1a]

Suspicions should have been aroused when the highly respected Chairman of the Senate Intelligence Committee, Bob Graham, voted against the Iraq war. He maintained that the evidence was "flimsy" and that our military sources should be focused on Afghanistan.

Some in Congress, like Senator John McCain, actually paved the way to war. In speeches, he said that a war in Iraq is the second phase of the war on terror and that there was "no doubt" that Saddam intended to use weapons of mass destruction against the United States and its allies. He linked Saddam to 9/11 and assured us that the "Iraqi people will greet us as liberators." On board the carrier Theodore Roosevelt he told the sailors "Next up Baghdad" (See Appendix III).

Congress did specify that the President support existing UN Security Council Resolutions and use diplomatic or other peaceful means. However, Congress did not seek out the advice of outside experts or the views of UN international inspectors who were on the ground in Iraq checking out U.S. intelligence.

These professional inspectors from many different countries found nothing to support the President's position—no evidence of a nuclear program or of biological weapons. The inspection teams conveyed this information to the U.N. publicly in two interim reports. The President invaded soon afterwards, forcing the inspectors to leave before they could finish their work (See chapter three).

During the war's build-up, the media did not challenge administration spokesmen or do their own work independently. Like Congress, they did not check administration claims against the findings of the onsite international inspectors. Their tendency was to rely on high-level administration sources and Iraqi defectors and exile groups who favored war.[2] The media's priority instead was to arrange for their own people to be imbedded with American troops so they could report directly from the war zone.

Although tens of thousands of illegal weapons were said to be in Iraq, no reporter ever obtained proof of a single one. For example, Secretary of Defense Rumsfeld briefed the Pentagon press people saying that he actually knew of many illegal weapons at two specific locations in Iraq. The press did not check out his statement with the findings of the arms inspectors inside Iraq.

Many of our largest newspapers and magazines published articles and editorials supporting the war in Iraq and the President's position on Iraq's illegal Weapons of Mass Destruction. Instead of being independent, they marched to the drumbeat of the administration like a state-run-media.

For example, *The New York Times* periodically reported that the threat from Iraq's was real and ominous. Later embarrassed, the *Times* apologized to its readers for not challenging the President's assumptions.[3] *The New Republic* magazine also expressed regret for its support of the war. The *Chicago Tribune* shockingly praised "the willingness of Congress to place its faith in Bush"

The Washington Post ran a major editorial in support of the war, assuming facts not in evidence. As their famous reporter Bob Woodard eventually acknowledged, his paper later downplayed the real evidence by putting it on the back pages. *The Washington Post* took an internal look at what happened, but did not apologize to its readership.

Among the few exceptions challenging the administration's assumptions were *Knight Ridder* (now the McClatchy Company) and the *Los Angeles Times*.

And, why didn't Congress and the media raise this particular question—if Iraq's thousands of Weapons of Mass Destruction actually existed, why would any sane person commit a hundred thousand U.S. personnel to a **land war** there and expose them to almost instant death? What were Congress and the media thinking about?

During the year-long run up to the war, three-fourths of the American people had the distinct impression that Saddam Hussein was directly linked to 9/11. How could the public have been so misled if the media and Congress had done their job? Where was the evidence?

Some of the factors that have turned the media from our guardians at the gate into stenographers are identified in the book, News Incorporated: Corporate Media Ownership and Its Threat to Democracy: [4]

- Federal policies that govern media ownership allowed a handful of corporate giants to swallow up independents and control the media industry.
- Now over eighty percent of independent newspapers are owned by corporate divisions of conglomerate companies, which are more concerned with profit and their political affiliation than with the need to keep the public well informed.
- Americans receive a censored version of reality and the watchdog of our democracy has become a docile instrument of government authority and big money.
- According to the media watchdog group, Fairness and Accuracy in Reporting, U.S. media outlets generally follow the Washington official line, frequently socialize with government officials and make large contributions to political parties, while receiving millions in return for running their campaign ads. In this incestuous culture, "news" is defined chiefly as the actions and statements of people in power.

Reporters dependent on "access" and "leaks" provided by official sources are too often unwilling to risk alienating these sources. Even the great Bob Woodward of Watergate fame became a stenographer early in the Bush administration until his third book, State of Denial, hit the book shelves.

We no longer have the hard-nosed, independent investigative reporting capability that made so many newsmen famous. News organizations today regularly become the beneficiaries of leaks from the administration. They protect their sources with a passion and no longer can be trusted to question actions and motives of their sources. The media is more obsessed with getting access to the reins of power than with getting at the truth.

The media's job is to question power, not succumb to it. In earlier times the media would dig into important issues, like Watergate, and stick with them until the truth was finally exposed and the public's interest protected. Today, reporters do hit-and-run jobs, like the thousands of piecemeal articles on 9/11 (See chapter two End Notes). No one followed up on these important pieces of information, conducted inquiring interviews, and put together the whole story.

Even to this day, there is no 9/11 accountability, although some 9/11 family victims have been pleading for it for over a decade. It's not that some enterprising journalist couldn't have pieced together the whole story. Rather, it's more likely that media managements feared confronting a sitting President with something as charged as 9/11 and life-and-death accountability.

Much of the media has relinquished its independence and acceded to government power and increasing control of big business. Under expanding corporate ownership, the media has a monetary incentive to play it safe and go along with a particular party's propaganda machine (or become a part of it) rather than inform the public in a fair and impartial manner.[5]

Two media professionals, Thomas Mann and Norman Ornstein, have been studying Washington politics and Congress for over 40 years and have written a new book, *IT's Even Worse Than it Looks: How the American Constitutional System Collided With the New Politics of Extremism.* They say the core of the problem rests with the Republican Party and the mainstream media's handling of it.

"The GOP has become an insurgent outlier in American politics. It is ideologically extreme; scornful of compromise; unmoved by conventional understandings of facts, evidence and science; and dismissive of the legitimacy of its political opposition."

"In the first two years of the Obama administration, nearly every presidential initiative met with vehement, rancorous and unanimous Republican opposition in the House and Senate, followed by efforts to delegitimize the results and repeal the policies."

"Republicans in the Senate have abused the confirmation process to block any and every nominee to posts … solely to keep laws that were legitimately enacted from being implemented."

Mann and Ornstein say the mainstream media's problem is trying to prove its lack of bias by taking refuge behind: "Both sides do it." They challenge use of this refuge by saying "a balanced treatment of an unbalance phenomenon distorts reality". Their advice to the press is to find out which politicians are telling the truth and look ahead to the consequences of voters' choices. Otherwise, our politics will only get worse.

In a 2011 article on "What Happened to All the Moderate Republicans," Time *Magazine* columnist Joe Klein accurately summed up the media's top priority today:

Our country is "facing a great challenge right now. We (the news media) really owe the public a good, smart, rigorous couple of years between now and election day, 2012."

Increasing Shift of Political Power to the Wealthy

Further endangering our democracy is a major shift of political power to the wealthy. According to the latest U.S. Census, the gap between the rich and poor during the last decade grew to the widest on record and represents the greatest disparity among Western industrialized nations.

According to *Forbes Magazine*, billionaires recently broke two records, their number and their combined wealth.

In 1992, only 33 of the top 400 income people in America paid less than twenty percent in taxes. In 2008, 253 did. According to IRS data, nearly 1500 millionaires and billionaires paid a zero tax in 2009. According to the independent Congressional Budget Office, the income scale of the top one percent grew 275 percent between 1979 and 2007. [6]

Warren Buffet, one of the richest men in the world, said that people working in his office pay almost double the tax rate that he does. He says that he knows many of the mega-rich and most of them wouldn't mind being told to pay more taxes. His position is that Congress should stop coddling the super-rich

Three important groups have urged that Bush tax cuts for the wealthy expire. They are the (1) Patriot Millionaires for Fiscal Strength, (2) Responsible Wealth and (3) Resource Generation (See Appendixes V and VI). Their positions are:

Patriot Millionaires – "Let the Bush tax cuts expire once and for all, and return the top marginal tax rate to the Clinton era levels." That was the message they sent to the congressional supercommittee during 2011 deliberations on deficit reduction.

Responsible Wealth – "The idea that business owners and wealthy individuals will not invest unless tax rates are low is a myth, and should not be used to justify tax cuts for the wealthy. We invest when there is a profit to be made, not because tax rates on our profits are low."

Resource Generation – "No budget cuts until we raise revenue from those of us who have benefited the most and have the greatest capacity to pay. It's all about taxes when you talk about unequal distribution of wealth in this country." They urged that higher tax money from the wealthy be used to rebuild infrastructure, smart grid, public transit and research initiatives. All of these will provide a foundation for future growth.

As noted in the Winner-Take-All of Politics book, American politics are being altered to benefit the few at the expense of the many. Another journalist put it differently: "The wealthy call the tune and politicians dance."[7] An interesting article by Economist, Richard Wolff, describes how the tax burden for the wealthiest Americans has shifted to those with less income.[8]

- The richest Americans have dramatically lowered their income tax burden since 1945 relative to the middle class and the poor.
- A vicious cycle is at work. Reduced taxes for the rich leave them more money to influence politicians and politics. That influence wins them still more money to put to political use, like gaining further tax reductions, loopholes in the tax code and subsidies.
- When the loss of tax revenue strains government budgets, the wealthy press politicians to cut public services and jobs.
- The money the wealthy save from taxes is sometimes invested in U.S. Treasury Bonds. Other taxpayers then have to pay more taxes to cover the interest on a rising debt which the wealthy helped to create in the first place.

According to *Wealth For Common Good. org.*, corporate taxes have declined from roughly thirty percent of the revenue collected by the government to about seven percent. Our top 100 companies paid on average of less than one-third of the corporate tax rate last year. Some paid in the medium range and others dodged their taxes completely or got huge refunds over the past five years.[9]

COMPANIES NOT PAYING FAIR SHARE OF TAX BURDEN

COMPANY	PROFIT	TAX Refund/Rebate/Break
Exxon Mobil	$19 Billion	$156 Million
Bank of America	$4.4 Billion	$1.9 Billion
General Electric	$26 Billion (last 5 years)	$4.1 Billion
Chevron	$10 Billion	$19 Million
Boeing	Unknown	$124 Million
Valero Energy	Unknown	$291 Million
Goldman Sacks	$2.3 Billion	Tax Rate paid – 1.1 Percent
Citigroup	$4 Billion	Paid No Tax
Conoco Phillips	$16 Billion (last 3 years)	$451 Million
Carnival Cruise	$11 Billion (last 5 years)	Tax Rate paid – 1.1 percent

In addition to tax loop holes, shelters and subsidies, there is the matter of tax havens for big business. A 2011 special on the CBS TV program, *60 Minutes*, reported that sixty billion a year is lost due to offshore tax dodging (called tax havens). Why should a big business be allowed to escape a fair share of its tax burden by simply moving its headquarters (on paper only) to a small country with a much lower tax rate?

A report released by Public Campaign at the end of 2011 shows that 30 big corporations actually spent more money lobbying the federal government between 2008 and 2010 than they paid in income taxes. In fact, all but one paid no taxes at all and instead got large rebates. Their lobbying expenditures ranged from $700 thousand to $84 million per company. General Electric in the table above led the way. The executive compensation of most companies increased significantly during the same period.[9a]

The UN ranks leading nations around the world in Democracy. Norway, Australia and the Netherlands lead the way. After an adjustment for income inequality, the U.S. dropped into twenty-third place.

The cost of the right-wing tax cuts since 2001 for the top five percent exceeds one trillion dollars. A serious trend in income inequality is underway and it is apparent that the wealthy are not paying their fair share of the tax burden.

The taxes we pay lay the foundation for a sound economy and wealth creation by funding such things as safe and efficient transportation (roads, bridges and railways), judicial courts, clean food and water, scientific research and protection from hurricanes, fires, criminals, and international terrorism.

Over the last century, untold trillions of taxpayer dollars have been invested in projects that benefitted all Americans, but especially the wealthy. Some illustrations that opened up business opportunities are:

- The Internet—Department of Defense.
- Miniaturization of electronics—Space Program.
- The Interstate Highway System.
- Education of the U.S. workforce.
- Diplomatic assistance and military protection in commerce around the globe.

These kinds of investments help business enterprises around the country get started and compete both here and abroad. Without these huge government investments many companies could not succeed. It seems clear that both businesses and high income people are obligated to share a greater tax burden and pay higher *effective* tax rates than the average American citizen.

As one *New York Times* columnist wrote, our economy should no longer bestow fabulous wealth on a tiny fraction of our population, while undermining the living standards of the middle class and crushing the poor. Only twice before in our history, has so much been held by so few – the late 1920's and the era of the robber barons in the 1880's.

He said that with severe income inequality, the general population does not consume enough to drive a modern economy. The U.S. economy needs to be rebalanced so that benefits are shared more widely and more equitably, and so that spending power across the entire population can sustain a flourishing economy.[10]

A strong middle class is the key to economic growth, not the right-wing trickle-down theory of economics. A strong middle class leads to a strong consumer base, increased education, long-term investments and better government. Even wealthy people do much better when there is a strong middle class.

These views were supported by a billionaire entrepreneur and venture capitalist in a December 2011 article (See Appendix VI). There, he directly challenges the right-wing rhetoric coming out of Congress.

"We've had it backwards for the last 30 years. Rich business people like me don't create jobs. Middle-class consumers do, and when they thrive, U.S. businesses grow and profit. That's why taxing the rich to pay for investments that benefit all is a great deal for both the middle class and the rich. So let's give a break to the true job creators. Let's tax the rich like we once did and use that money to spur growth by putting purchasing power back in the hands of the middle class. And let's remember that capitalists without customers are out of business."

The danger down the road is that our freedom will be jeopardized by a nation run by a relatively small group of wealthy people. America invests heavily in the future and offers opportunities for all. As Oliver Wendell Holmes said, "Taxes are what we pay for a civilized society." We should all pay our dues. Those who do not are cheating those who do.

Overhauling Our Electoral System

Election financing of elections has promoted corruption and imperils our democracy. Huge sums are required to win elections, and to survive, politicians are sorely tempted to appease big money interests. Massive contributions are transformed into legislative favors – a form of "legalized bribery." The money party, not the people's party, dominates politics.[11]

The situation can only get worse because of record expenditures now required to win elections. This record is, in part, due to a Supreme Court 5-4 decision that enables corporations and individuals to make unlimited contributions on behalf of political parties and their candidates without disclosing the source. Elected officials who stand up against corporations on particular issues now face the prospect of huge funding against them during the next election.

The fundamental issues at stake are (1) whether our system of selecting presidents is under siege and (2) will the 2012 election and follow-on ones reflect the will of the people?

The Citizens United Debacle

The Supreme Court majority view in the Citizens United Decision is referred to below as the "Roberts 5" and its monumental Dissent is referred to as the "Stevens 4." The discussion that follows is based on an analysis of and material drawn from the Roberts 5 and Stevens 4 parts of the Decision plus three articles critiquing that Decision.

Two of three articles are by two authors who collaborated. James Marc Leas is a former engineer, a prolific inventor and now, a patent lawyer. Rob Hager is an attorney with long experience in public interest litigation. The third article is by Elizabeth Drew, a distinguished journalist, TV commentator, author of 14 books and recipient of many honorary degrees.

The Roberts 5 concluded that Congress could not provide any regulation at all of independent election expenditures and that freedom of speech in the First Amendment to the Constitution provides the absolute right to hear corporation ads.

The Roberts 5 position is that voters must be free to obtain information from diverse sources in order to determine how to cast their votes. Otherwise, there is censorship. They believe that any undue influence generated by large expenditures is outweighed by the loss of democratic process resulting from restrictions upon full and free public discussion.

The Stevens 4 Dissent concluded that members of Congress, with actual experience in politics over the past century, have demonstrated a recurrent need to (1) regulate corporate participation in candidate elections, (2) prevent corruption, (3) sustain the active and alert responsibility of individual citizens, (4) protect the interests of shareholders of corporations and (5) preserve individual citizens' confidence in government.

Our two authors' position is that our founding fathers rightly understood that Congress would be far more subject to popular pressure to maintain election integrity than would the appointed-for-life members of the court. By taking up a case and overturning a law that provides for election integrity, they say the court *infringed on a power specifically assigned under the Constitution to Congress,* thereby undermining the separation of powers.

They believe the public has a profound and compelling interest in preventing the death of representative democracy by allowing continued auction of its elections and laws to wealthy corporations. Corporations profit from the government policies and government contracts they receive in exchange for their payoffs to and for politicians. Eventually, individuals will lose faith in their capacity as citizens, to influence public policy and hold officials accountable. This will diminish their willingness to participate in the democratic process.

Our two authors go on to say that the Court misinterpreted the language of the First Amendment on freedom of speech as providing such absolute right to hear corporation ads as to overshadow the public's greater interest in preventing private money from corrupting elections and government. They contend that flaws in the Decision provide grounds to overturn all Supreme Court decisions on private money in politics (See Appendix VII).

The Stevens 4 monumental Dissent reveals flaws in the decision, as well as flaws in decision-makers themselves.

FLAWS WITH CITIZENS UNITED DECISION AND ITS DECIDERS

DECISION FLAWS	DECIDERS' FLAWS
Contrary to the decision, there is a serious distinction between corporate and human speakers in freedom of speech.	If anyone knows the financial failings of political contests, it's members of Congress, not Supreme Court Judges.
Direct contributions are limited, but not corporate ones.	Judges, without political background, had little grounding in election evidence and experience.
System that forces corporations to use shareholders' money both to maintain access to and avoid retribution from elected officials may ultimately prove more harmful than beneficial to corporations. It can impose a kind of implicit tax.	Court acted on issues not properly presented or properly brought before it. No record of burdens of existing law submitted before court.
Allows corporate people to use other peoples' money to support candidates they have made no decision to support or to oppose candidates they have made no decision to oppose.	It is members of the court, not public listeners themselves, who have agitated for more corporate speech.
Investments in corporations can be used to undermine the investor's political convictions.	Five justices, unhappy with limited case, changed it to have opportunity to change election laws.
Stockholders not able, in practice, to confront political ads adverse to their beliefs.	Previously rejected dissents of earlier cases used in majority opinion. The only changes were the composition of the court.
Profitability of corporation is at stake, not the public good. Few natural persons can match their resources.	Their partisan overreaching decision shows great disrespect for its co-equal branch, Congress.
Promotes corporate power at the expense of the individual.	
Real people of nation should determine how they will be governed.	

The author of the Roberts 5 Decision, Justice Kennedy, said "independent expenditures" in favor of candidates "do not give rise to corruption or the appearance of corruption". Actually, candidates are likely to have a hand in setting up Super PACs and their previous associates may also be put in charge of them. This has already occurred in the 2012 presidential campaigns.

A previous decision (Buckley vs. Vales) did equate spending of money to free speech. However, as Elizabeth Drew notes, that decision applied to "limited" contributions, not the unlimited ones now permitted in the Citizens United decision.

Our two authors' view is the court broke new ground and reversed clear precedent while failing to strike a rationale and principled balance between the negligible speech value of private money in elections and the harm such private money causes to a democratic form of government. They believe money in politics must be regulated because of the severe harm it can do to our democracy.

Our two authors note that the Roberts 5 used this case to rewrite the law relating to campaign expenditures by for-profit corporations and unions. Yet, these two entities were not party to the case – a violation of the Constitution's "case and Controversy" requirement.

The Stevens 4 Dissent stressed that a corporation or union can always speak for itself and would be held accountable by its shareholders and members for doing so. On the other hand, money in their treasuries should not be siphoned off for political purposes (without disclosure) to support or destroy a particular candidate.

Under our Constitution citizens, not corporations, have the final say—the legislators are their spokesmen. The people through their votes determine the destiny of the nation. In his dissent to the recent Supreme Court decision, Justice Stevens said:

> *"At bottom, the Court's opinion is thus a rejection of the common sense of the American people, who have recognized a need to prevent corporations from undermining self government since the founding, and who have fought against the distinctive corrupting potential of corporate electioneering since the days of Theodore Roosevelt. It is a strange time to repudiate that common sense. While American democracy is imperfect, few outside the majority of this Court would have thought its flaws included a dearth of corporate money in politics."*

The Montana Supreme Court has defied the Citizens United decision by refusing to overturn its Corrupt Practices Act for state candidates and political parties. [12] Its defiance was subsequently blocked by the Supreme Court pending final disposition of the case. Vermont and some other states are also in strong opposition. They have called for a constitutional amendment to undo the U.S. Supreme Court decision.

There are three alternatives being debated to reverse the Supreme Court decision, each one controversial. One is suggested by a Harvard ethics expert who has studied the problem for well over a decade. In a recent book, he says that perhaps the only way to cope with our entrenched political system and boundaries set by Supreme Court decisions is for our states to petition for a Constitutional Convention. [13]

The second approach is for Congress to act. Democratic members of Congress have introduced constitutional amendments to overturn the Citizens United decision and restore the ability of Congress to regulate campaign financing.

One of these is the Saving American Democracy Amendment. It does three things: (a) clarifies that corporations are not natural persons, (b) limits the amount of money individuals can spend to influence elections and (c) requires all political action committees to disclose sources of their donations. [14] The Senate and House sponsors contend that:

> *"Every member of the Senate, every member of the House, in the back of their minds will be asking this: If I cast a vote this way, if I take on some big-money interest, am I going to be punished? Will a huge amount of money be unleashed in my state?"*

Super majorities will be required to pass a constitutional amendment to reverse the decision. Partisanship in both the current Congress and state houses makes the first two approaches seem unlikely and untimely unless there is overwhelming public support.

The third alternative is one proposed by our two authors. They contend that an immediate solution is available based on an ordinary majority vote in Congress.

They believe that the Supreme Court has overstepped its judicial powers and intruded on congress's legislative powers to regulate and judge elections as provided in **Article I, Sections 4 and 5** of the Constitution. They believe further that members of Congress and an aroused public can demand that Congress use its existing powers under **Article III, Section 2** of the Constitution to restore the traditional limits on court jurisdiction over political questions of private money in elections (See appendix VII).

Our two authors oppose a constitutional amendment to address private interest financing of elections because it would legitimatize the Supreme Court having jurisdiction over election financing and divert from a solution already in the Constitution to more effectively solve the problem.

In conclusion, our two authors contend that Congress can pass legislation reversing the court's decisions that corrupt elections and remove Supreme Court jurisdiction over financing of election campaigns. Congress and the states would then be free to pass laws removing or limiting private money from election campaigns.

Finally, they maintain that this direct route to restoring government of, by and for the people removes the court's power to find other creative vehicles to corrupt elections, and is now available without a constitutional amendment.

By re-establishing the bar on court jurisdiction over election financing, it may be possible for Congress to limit private interest money to relatively small donations matched by public funding. As Elizabeth Drew notes, this would enable candidates to have a floor of sufficient financing to assure a competitive race if the candidate can attract sufficient donors.

An excerpt from a Bill Moyers forward to the book, Corporations Are Not People, sums up the problem.

America has a long record of conflict with corporations. Wealth acquired under capitalism is in and of itself no enemy to democracy, but wealth armed with political power – power to choke off opportunities for others to rise, power to subvert public purposes and deny public needs – is a proven danger to the "general welfare" proclaimed in the Preamble to the Constitution as one of the justifications for America's existence.

Further discussion of this decision's credibility can be found in a section on Legitimacy of Supreme Court Decisions that concludes this chapter.

Partial Public Financing

Partial public financing would take political power from the wealthy and return it to the people. It encourages candidates to raise small dollar donations from average Americans and receive a public match. The public match is limited for each donor, but many more citizens would be involved in assuring our democracy works for all.

Public financing of elections is being used in some advanced democracies and is being tried out here in Arizona, Connecticut, Maine and North Carolina. New York State is seriously considering this approach for local elections.

Lawton Chiles earned two terms in the Senate and as Governor of Florida by walking the state and limiting campaign contributions to small amounts. Today's candidates have the added power of the Internet to seek contributions as well as time from their supporters.

If we had *free broadcast time from our public airways* and *public financing,* more incumbents would be challenged and more candidates from the middle class could compete for office. Two thirds of Americans and at least 100 former and current members of Congress have supported public financing.

To qualify for public funding, a candidate would need to first demonstrate competence by raising small dollar amounts from voters across his or her voting district. In April 2011, Senator Richard Durbin and Representative John Larson introduced the Fair Election Now Act. It would help candidates remain free from corporate interests by providing public money for their campaigns, if they first demonstrate voter interest by raising small-dollar contributions.

Making Elections More Open and Competitive

Incumbents are often re-elected to Congress unless the public has reached the point of outrage, but by then, the damage is done. We shouldn't have to suffer a failed presidency or a national economic crisis in order to unseat incumbents.

Among incumbent advantages are name recognition, voting districts drawn in their favor and established funding sources. They call on contributors who benefit from their favors and voting record. Incumbents also receive money allocated by their political party.

State districts for congressional representatives are drawn to favor candidates of a particular party in power and/or reelection of the incumbent. This unfair advantage can last a lifetime for an incumbent. True competition between political candidates is lacking and moderates and independents have less chance of being elected to office.[15] The public may wind up with little to choose from in the way of candidates to represent them.

The occupants of these seats can be extreme partisans who are unable to find common ground with the other party on matters of national importance, like job creation, deficits, taxes and safety net programs. Today, a national crisis has to erupt before partisans in Congress are willing to compromise, and even then it may not happen.

In addition, the U.S. needs to replace the state by state electoral system with a popular vote to decide presidential elections. Currently from 8 to a maximum of 14 states (referred to as battleground states) decide who will be our next president. The votes of some 200-300 million people of other states don't matter.

Legitimacy of U.S. Supreme Court Decisions

Our legal system was designed to set law apart from politics. The idea was, in return for life-time tenure, justices would exercise judgment independently and be free from the powerful and not cultivate them in any way. The Supreme Court has moved further to the right and departed from this important principle on at least three occasions—each one changing the direction of our country.

First, in a very unwise decision, the Supreme Court disrupted our government by allowing a baseless civil sexual harassment suit to go forward against a sitting President. This played right into the hands of a right-wing conspiracy to reclaim the White House. In addition, the Court gave this conspiracy an **unconstitutional** weapon—the Independent Council function—which was a fourth branch of government with unlimited powers and budgets (See chapter one).

Second, in the presidential election that followed, the Supreme Court interfered with Florida's right to a full vote recount, and the right- wing conspirators finally achieved their goal – the White House.

The Florida Supreme Court demanded a statewide recount of the Bush/Gore election results because (1) of a minuscule difference in total vote count and (2) the true intent of many thousands of Florida voters had not been properly recorded due to a poorly designed ballot.

The Florida's court's decision was appealed to the Supreme Court. The high court immediately stopped the recount and decided a few days later, in effect, to appoint Bush as President. This prevented Florida from determining, as best it could, who actually had won the election.[16]

In its highly unusual 5-4 **unsigned** opinion, the Supreme Court created its own criteria and said there must be a state-wide standard across the many Florida counties to determine voter intent. However, state counties often have different voting systems and different ways of counting votes. Many state elections across the country would not qualify under this Supreme Court decision. Basically, a recount of voter intent was a judgment call on the part of professional judges examining the ballot, and the recount should have been continued.[17]

A later recount of ballots by an independent media consortium of a dozen newspapers reported that Vice-President Gore would have won a statewide recount, the one demanded by the Florida Supreme Court. A *New York Times* study found that poorly designed ballots in two counties cost Gore over 8,000 votes and would have made a difference in the outcome.[18]

Reportedly, one of the Republican-appointed Supreme Court Justices, awaiting an urgently needed retirement (Sandra Day O'connor), was visibly shaken because the Florida recount might allow her impending vacancy to be appointed by a President of the opposite political party.

According to Justice Steven's dissent the loser was not Vice-President Gore, but instead:

> **"... the nation's confidence in the judge as an impartial guardian of the rule of law."**

The Supreme Court overstepped its judicial authority by interfering with a state election contest for the first time in American history and essentially shutting it down. It should have allowed a full recount in Florida and let voters and professional judges decide the outcome. Even the Supreme Court sensed something was awry and limited its decision to this one case and has never cited it again.[19]

Questioned on this Decision in a March 2012 speech at Wesleyan University, Supreme Court Justice Scalia said incorrectly that: "It was a 7-2 decision. It wasn't even close ... Get over it." Although 4 moderate judges differed on how to fix the Florida recount, they all disagreed with the Scalia 5 right-wing judges. So, a 5-4 Supreme Court decision stopped the recount, chose the winner of the 2000 election and cost the nation dearly.

Third, and even more dangerous to our democracy, is the recent Supreme Court decision that overturns a hundred years of law and could be the death of our democracy. In Citizens United v. Federal Election Commission, the high court allows corporations, including foreign-controlled ones, to spend undisclosed and unlimited funds in political contests.

> *The case came to the Supreme Court as a limited question about interpreting a federal campaign-finance statute. In an aggressive act of judicial activism, the conservative majority made the case a constitutional matter and the signature of the Roberts court. Sweeping aside established precedents that had not been challenged and inserting itself into politics, the conservative majority unleashed unlimited corporate and other money into American politics and gave the Republican Party a large advantage in fund-raising.*
>
> *The Court and the Next President*
> *New York Times Editorial*
> *Oct. 28, 2011*

This decision means that secret big money interests can corrupt the political process anywhere, thousands of miles away from the source of the money. It also means that the value of an individual citizen's vote will diminish dramatically.

Following the Supreme Court decision, right-wing leadership in Congress immediately blocked a Disclose Act that would have required all political donors be publically identified.

The Court's new decision opened the flood gates for hundreds of millions of dollars to influence the 2010 midterm elections. A number of individual election contests were affected. It has also emboldened previously hesitant wealthy donors to pour money into tax-exempt groups.

Most of the outside money was funneled through a small number of groups, led by the U.S. Chamber of Commerce and two Karl Rove-affiliated operations. Most of the groups were funded by a small number of corporations and wealthy individuals. And their spending had a disproportionate influence on the election. They were able to focus their efforts in close and strategically important races ... They were also free to run vicious attack ads without the even the reputational harm that attaches to candidates who run negative ads.

Organizations associated with the two Karl Rove groups and the Kock brothers' billionaires plan to spend $240 and 200 million respectively in the 2012 presidential election. These amounts alone exceed the total spent in the last presidential campaign by Republican presidential candidate Senator John McCain.[20] Research of historical statements made on this issue should have given the Supreme Court pause.

"The first thing to understand is the difference between the natural person and the fictitious person called a corporation. They differ in the purpose for which they are created, in the strength which they possess, and in the restraints under which they act.

"Man is the handiwork of God and was placed upon earth to carry out a Divine purpose; the corporation is the handiwork of man and created to carry out a money-making policy.

"There is comparatively little difference in the strength of men; a corporation may be one hundred, one thousand, or even one million

times stronger than the average man. Man acts under the restraints of conscience, and is influenced also by a belief in a future life. A corporation has no soul and cares nothing about the hereafter..."

William Jennings Bryan, in his address to the Ohio 1912 Constitutional Convention

The President of Public Citizen put it this way, "Corporations have perpetual life, they have no conscience, they can't be imprisoned, and they are driven by a single objective – pursuit of profit."

A study, conducted by the respected Hart Institute Associates, found that four out of five Americans sharply disapprove of the Supreme Court's decision and support a constitutional amendment to reverse the ruling. They found substantial support across party lines to make clear that corporations do not have the same rights as people. According to the survey, the public also has little faith in our current political system.[21]

Common Cause has petitioned the Department of Justice to investigate the impartiality of two of the Supreme Court Judges - Justices Antonin Scalia and Clarence Thomas - involved in the Citizens United 5-4 decision. They attended or were featured at political strategy meetings sponsored by a corporation (Koch Industries) that raises and spends millions to defeat Democrats and elect Republicans.[22]

Because impartial decision-making is so essential to success of the Supreme Court, it has been held that due process is violated when a judge participates in a case involving a party that helped him obtain his judgeship (Caperton v. A.T. Massey). Notwithstanding that decision, Justice Thomas sat in judgment of the controversial Citizens United case although that organization had spent at least $100,000 in support of his nomination to the Supreme Court.[23]

Thomas also repeatedly failed during his years on the Supreme Court to properly report substantial financial income (at least$1.6 million) received by his wife from a right-wing think tank. In September 2011, three groups (the Alliance for Justice, Common Cause and over 20 lawmakers in Congress) asked the Judicial Conference of the United States to investigate whether Justice Thomas violated the Ethics in Government Act.[24]

In addition, Judge Thomas's wife has been an outspoken critic of the Obama administration, helped to lead the Tea Party from its inception and is the founder of a group of donors who endorsed Republican candidates in about a dozen states.

On all these matters, Justice Thomas faces a call for disbarment from his home state of Missouri for multiple violations of rules of professional conduct.[25]

The Protect Our Elections Group has filed a second bar complaint against Justice Thomas for his failure to disqualify himself from the "Citizens United" case and for hiding the fact that this organization had supported his nomination to the Supreme Court.[26]

A leading historian of the Supreme Court, Lucas Powe, said Justice Scalia "is taking political partisanship to levels not seen in over half a century." The Director of Alliance for Justice has expressed concern about both Justices Scalia and Thomas attending political meetings and events. The Director specifically had in mind those sponsored by billionaires, like the Koch brothers, who are now taking full advantage of the new decision allowing unlimited and secret corporate contributions.[27]

A key issue is whether Scalia or Thomas or both should have recused themselves from the Citizen United case. The same question is being posed on Judge Thomas's upcoming participation in the widely anticipated decision on constitutionality of the new health care reform law.

His wife received about two-thirds of a million dollars over several years from a foundation opposed to that law. Seventy-four Democrats have signed a letter asking Justice Thomas not to participate in that case on the grounds of an appearance of conflict of interest.[28]

In October 2011, a large group of Democratic lawmakers asked the House and Senate Judiciary Committees to investigate a number of "ethical lapses" by Justice Thomas, including air travel, yacht stays and other gifts from wealthy supporters. The letter questions Thomas's "ability to retain his seat." Over 200,000 people across the U.S. have signed a petition calling for his resignation.

The ethics code for lower courts does not apply to the Supreme Court. A group of more than a hundred law professors from around the country has asked Congress to extend an ethical code of conduct to the Supreme

Court for the first time in history. The idea is to have enforceable rules to protect the integrity of the Supreme Court.[29]

Representative Chris Murphy has called for Judiciary Committee hearings on escalating reports of unethical behavior by Supreme Court Justices. He introduced the Supreme Court Transparency and Disclosure Act requiring a judicial ethics code for the Supreme Court. Right-wing leaders in Congress have not signed on to this bill and it is unlikely to go anywhere.

Two New York Times editorials question: (1) why Justices are left free to decide whether they should withdraw from a case and (2) why the Supreme Court does not operate on the same principles that apply to all other judges in the country. The editorials suggested that:

- **A justice be required to explain publicly any decision to recuse or not.**

- **A group of justices review the recusal decision and have the power to overrule it.**[30]

In an end of the year 2011 Supreme Court report, Chief Justice Roberts opposed this on the grounds that other justices could affect the outcome of the case by selecting who may participate. His statement simply acknowledges the partisanship and questionable ethics that goes on among members of the court. In February 2012, he refused to adopt an ethical code of conduct for the Court.

Since the Citizens United decision, right-wing groups have received many millions of dollars from banks, health insurers and other business interests. These businesses will expect returns on their investment. If they did not, they would not make the investments in the first place.

Unless Citizens United is overturned, Corporations will have the right to influence election outcomes anywhere in the United States.[27] They can use millions of dollars to defeat candidates that support legislation threatening their bottom line. Corporate influences on elections have been referred to as "a cancer in our political system and a "major political crisis."[31]

Conclusions and Remedies

A few huge corporations now own the vast majority of our newspapers, and radio and TV stations. Their profit taking and political affiliations conflict with their independent role and duty as our fourth estate to keep the public well informed. In some cases they border on a propaganda machine. This situation constitutes a threat to our democracy.

Too often the media do not challenge the reins of power until it is too late to undo the damage and reverse course. Its investigative function has nearly vanished. Public hearings are needed to inquire into the overall conduct of the media in our democracy. These hearings should thoroughly investigate whether a few large conglomerates are using the media for political gain and interfering with the freedom of the press.

Some of the best critics of what has gone wrong are members of the media itself. They and others should have the opportunity to come forward and express their views at public hearings. Some issues that should be covered are real independence from those being reported on, excessive concentration of media ownership, and conflicts of interest between ownership and the people's right to know.

Congress will do a better job when its members are kept informed by a free and independent media, and when congressional members have enough financial independence at election time to speak freely for their constituents. The media, in turn, will do a better job when Congress questions administration policy and investigates potential wrong doings.

When these two institutions feed off each other, they become more effective, while keeping the public better informed. A knowledgeable public will be in a better position to influence public policy and choose their most qualified representatives and national leaders.

Working together, these three elements—Congress, the media, and a well-informed public – can strengthen our democracy and serve as an essential check and balance on the executive branch of government.

The wealthy and big businesses are enjoying the fruits of our democracy, but are not sharing in the cost of maintaining it. To assure that corporations and the wealthy are paying their fair share of the tax burden, Congress needs to reform and greatly simplify the tax code and eliminate tax loopholes, tax subsidies, tax havens and tax avoidance schemes.

The best way to correct income inequality in this country is to get big moneyed interests out of politics. We need elections of, by, and for the people – not ones paid for by giant corporations and the wealthy. Corporations should not be allowed to drown out the voices of the people. Further, it is demeaning for members of Congress to have to beg for money and spend so much time in office doing so.

Limiting donations to small amounts matched by public financing represents a historic opportunity for politicians to end their endless money chase that favors big donors and corporate lobbyists. No longer would their actions in Congress have to be heavily influenced by contributions to survive the ever increasing cost of elections.

We need to reverse the Supreme Court Citizens United decision and explore a new system for electing officials that:

- Removes the overwhelming influence of big money and bans anonymous political contributions.
- Promotes more candidates to compete for office and permits partial public financing for worthy candidates.
- Requires States to (1) use open primaries and (2) have an independent entity redraw voting districts without bias or favoritism.
- Increases voter turnout and deter voter suppression through use of a modern system of *universal voter registration* (See chapter eight).
- Elects presidents on the basis of a national popular vote, not on a few battleground states, like Ohio and Florida.

Partisan politics have gotten so bad that our judicial system seems to have caught the virus. Some judicial decisions across the country seem political in nature favoring Republicans or Democrats depending on the judges' party affiliation. Ultimately, some of these cases wind up in the Supreme Court. Partisanship is affecting its decisions too and doing irreversible damage to its role as an impartial decision maker.

We need judges who won't twist the law in order to privilege the already powerful. And, we need a Supreme Court that serves as a model for other courts across the nation. Remedial action must be taken because (1) the Supreme Court is largely unaccountable to anyone and (2) American citizens have no further right of appeal from its decisions.

There have been a number of unwise Supreme Court decisions from an unelected and unaccountable body. These decisions have turned our country in the wrong direction several times. Things may get worse because the current Supreme Court is the first one not to have a justice who previously served in elected office. And its members have about one-third the experience in private practice as previous courts.

Justices today are living a much longer life than those who lived when our founders created their branch of government over two centuries ago. Without a great deal of practical wisdom, they can lose touch with reality over time. Suggested remedies are that:

- The Supreme Court make every effort to remove itself from politics if it wants to have its decisions viewed as legitimate and retain permanent life-time appointments.
- The House and Senate Judiciary Committees hold public hearings on the Supreme Court decision-making process and demand that the Court:
  - Adopt a code of ethics,
  - Establish a system for recusing themselves when there is a conflict of interest, and
  - Discontinue their activities in overt political affairs.
- Carefully consider future appointments and subject them to term limits, like 12 or 16 years, if conditions do not improve.

In addition, Congress should consider impeachment of Justice Thomas for improper conduct.

ENDNOTES

1. "Empire at the End of Decadence," Charles Blow, *New York Times*, Feb. 18, 2011. "IMK bombshell: Age of America Nears End," Brett Arenda, *MarketWatch*, April 25, 2011.

1a. "Simply the Worst, Maureen Dowd", New York Times, Feb. 12, 2011.

2. "Where was the Media?" *Center for American Progress Report*, Feb. 11, 2004. "Now They Tell Us," *The New York Review of Books*, Feb. 26, 2004.34.

3. "New York Times ombudsman prints withering critique of Iraq coverage," *U.S. National*, May 30, 2004.

4. News Incorporated: Corporate Media Ownership and its Threat to Democracy, Elliot Cohen, Prometheus Books, 2005. "Who Owns the Media," Free Press, Jan. 2 2005.

5. "Howard Dean: Fox News is a well-funded, Right wing Propaganda Organization," Matt Schneider, Mediaite, April, 3, 2011.

6. "For Our Top 400 Taxpayers, a Near Record Year," Sam Pizzigati, *Campaign For America's Future*, May 14, 2011. "Stop Coddling the Super-Rich", Warren Buffett, NY Times, August 14, 2011. Author Stephen King: "Why Aren't the Rich Like Me Paying More Taxes?," *Afl-cionowblog*, March 10, 2011. "Rebuilding the American Dream by Returning to Fairer Tax Rates", Lee Harris, United for a Fair Economy, Aug. 7, 2011. "Money and Company", L.A. Times, Aug. 8, 2011.

7. "When Democracy Weakens," Bob Herbert, *New York Times*, Feb. 11, 2011.

8. "How the Rich Soaked the Rest of Us," Richard Wolff, *Truthout*, March 2, 2011. "The Great Switch by the Super Rich: How Wealthy Americans Started Paying So Little in Taxes," Robert Reich, *AlterNet*, May 21, 2011.

9. "Release: Tax Time? Not for Giant Corporations," *Newsroom*: U.S. Senator Bernie Sanders, March 27, 2011. "What Are We Doing Subsidizing Corporations through Tax Giveaways?" Paul Buchheit, *Buzzflash At Truthout*, March 31, 2011. "2/3rds of U.S. corporations

Pay Zero Federal Taxes," Allison Kilkenny, *The Nation*, March 27, 2011. "How G.E. made 5.1 billion in the U.S. tax free," David Kocieniewski, *New York Times*, March 24, 2011. "Super rich see federal taxes drop dramatically," Stephen Ohlemacher, *Associated Press*, April 17, 2011.

9a. "For Hire: Lobbyists or the 99%? How Corporations Pay More for Lobbyists Than in Taxes", A report by Public Campaign, December 2011. "Between 2008 And 2010, Thirty Big Corporations Spent More Lobbying Washington Than They Paid in Income Taxes", Zaid Jilani, thinkprogress.org/economy, Dec. 7, 2011.

10. "A Recovery's Long Odds," Bob Herbert, *New York Times*, Sept. 13, 2010. "Growth and the middle class," David Madland, *Democracy, A Journal of Ideas*, Spring 2011. "Actually, The Rich Don't Create Jobs, We Do," Yana, *Truthout*, May 14, 2011

11. "Getting Serious About Corruption," David Sirota, *Tom Paine.com*, Nov. 20, 2006. "Public financing," *reviewjournal.com*, Dec. 1, 2010. "Campaign finance reformers carry on without their leader," Tom Hamburger and David Salvage, *Washington Bureau, latimes.com*, Jan.3, 2011.

12. "Montana State Supreme Court: Citizens United Not Welcome Here", Sam Ferguson, Truthout. Jan. 4, 2012.

13. "Republic, Lost: How Money Corrupts Congress – and a Plan to Stop It, Lawrence Lessig, Grand Central Publishing, 2011. "Has a Harvard Professor Mapped Out the Next Step for Occupy Wall Street?" Alesh Houdek, the Atlantic, Dec. 29, 2011.

14. "Fact sheet" issued by Senator Sanders on Dec. 8, 2011.

15. "Redistricting, When will Virginians say 'enough', Our elected leaders could have introduced true political democracy", James Ukrop and Bryson Powell, Richmond Times Dispatch, June 12, 2011.

16. "Precedent And Prologue," Jeffery Toobin, *The New Yorker*, Dec. 6, 2010. "10 Years After Bush Vs. Gore, What's Changed?" Liane Hansen, *NPR*, Dec. 12, 2010. <u>The Vote: Bush, Gore, and the Supreme Court</u>, David Strauss, University of Chicago Press, 2001. "Florida election recount," *Wikipedia*. "Unequal Protection: The Court Takes the Presidency", Thom Hartmann, Truthout, July 18, 2011.

17. Ibid

18. Ibid

19. Ibid

20. "We got it wrong: Citizens United fallout is much worse than we had anticipated," Robert Weisman, President, of Public Citizen, *The Sacramento Bee*, Jan 24, 2011. "Corporate contributions have surged for new Republican leaders in the House," Dan Eggen and T.W. Farnam, *Washington Post*, Jan. 22, 2011. "Stanching the flow of corporate dollars into campaigns", Katrina vanden Heuvel, Washington Post, Nov. 8, 2011. *"The Washington Current"*, Senator Boxer, March 29, 2011.

21. "Survey: Four in Five Americans Support Amendment to Overturn Citizens United," *On The Hill*, Jan. 22, 2011.

22. "Scalia, Thomas and Citizens United," Jeanne Cummings, *Politico*, Jan. 19, 2011. "Clarence Thomas Faces Call For His Disbarment," *Legal Schnauzer*, March 2, 2011. "Clarence Thomas Must Go", William Rivers Pitt, Truthout, June 23, 2011. "More Ethics Trouble for Clarence Thomas", Stephanie Meneimer, Mother Jones, Sept. 14, 2011. "Justice Thomas failed to disclose that Citizen United spent more than $100,000 on ads, supported his nomination," *ProtectOurElections.org*, Feb. 18, 2011. "You Get the Judges You Pay For", Erwin Chemerinsky and James Sample, New York Times, April 17, 2011.

23. Ibid

24. Ibid

25. Ibid

26. Ibid

27. "Professors ask Congress for an ethics code for Supreme Court," Jeffrey Smith, *Washington Post*, Feb. 23, 2011.

28. "House Democrats say Justice Thomas should recuse himself in health-care case," Felicia Sonmez, *44 Politics and Policy*, Feb. 9, 2011. "Clarence Thomas failed to report Wife's income, watchdog says," Kim Greiger, *Washington Bureau, Latimes.com*. "Rep. Earl Blumenauer, Democrats, demand ethics probe of Supreme Court Justice Clarence Thomas", Charles Pope, The Oregonian, October 5, 2011.

29. "Professors ask Congress for an ethics code for Supreme Court," Jeffrey Smith, *Washington Post*, Feb. 23, 2011.

30. "Politics and the Court" and "The Supreme Court Recusal Problem", *New York Times Editorials*, Feb. 4, 2011 and Nov. 30, 2011.
31. "A 'Summit for the People,' Call for Action on Citizens United," James Russell, *Truthout Report*, Jan. 24, 2011.

Chapter Eight

―――――――

REPAIRING OUR SYSTEM OF POLITICS

Our political system is broken. Only the public and electoral reform can fix it. In the meantime, other advanced countries have already surpassed us in things like education, economic growth and clean energy technologies. The 20th century belonged to America; the 21st will not – unless we change our system of politics and strengthen our democracy.

The U.S. intelligence community, a coalition of seventeen activities in the executive branch, is exploring our country's future and, while that study is still in progress, it indicates that an eventual decline in our leadership role will occur. The intelligence community asked an independent journalist (David Ignatius of the *Washington Post*) to critique their work. He had more hope than the intelligence community did and believes that "the nation's chronic weakness is its political system, which is approaching dysfunction."[1]

The basic concept of democracy is that each of us should have a voice in the decisions that affect our lives. We live in a representative democracy and must abide by its decisions. Free elections of our leaders provide legitimacy to the winner and the right to rule. Our country was built on the basic principle that, when a particular political party is defeated at the ballot box, it must pay a price for the public good. Once intense campaigning and political infighting are over, our democracy demands that we pull together and support a newly-elected President from either party.

We have only one President at a time, and he or she speaks for all the people. The losing party becomes the loyal opposition, not the enemy; the President represents all the people, not just his own party. Minority leaders in Congress are expected to become team players, especially in times of national crisis.

Political parties out of power obviously are anxious to find ways to regain it. As we have seen in previous chapters, when they do so at any cost, they weaken our nation and undermine our democracy. The only defense the American people have is to judge how reckless this political behavior is and act accordingly. When Edward R. Murrow made his famous broadcast that led to the demise of Senator McCarthy, he gave this advice to his staff: "No one can terrorize a nation, unless **we** are his accomplices."

Differing Characteristics of the Political Parties

The characteristics of our two major parties differ in important respects. The right-wing led **Republican Party** has fewer supporters, but more money to finance elections. It has better party discipline than the Democrats and usually operates as one body whether in or out of power (until the Tea Party came along). Republican policies have tended to favor big business and high income people. Republicans long for smaller government and reduced taxes.

In earlier times, the Republican Party was more progressive. Its leaders, like Presidents Abraham Lincoln and Theodore Roosevelt, were moderates. In recent decades, the Party has gradually been taken over by its right wing and corporate power. Moderates have been exiled and new ones are not welcomed unless they reside in a heavily Democratic district.

Right-wing leaders are tough; they have the courage of their convictions and a well-organized attack machine. They rely on money, the mass media, fear tactics, and a strong messaging machine. They frame their messages better than Democrats and drill them repeatedly into the minds of low information voters.

A long-time Republican staffer who served in both the House and Senate observed: "The right wing is not a synonym for conservative and not even a true variant of conservatism—although it will opportunistically borrow conservative themes, as required". You will find other interesting comments from him later in this chapter.

Right-wing extremists tend to think of their political adversaries, not as patriots with differing views, but as un-American.[1a] The right wing is composed of three groups, the ultra or hardcore right which has extremist beliefs and can be violent (about 10% of the American electorate). The second group is conservative by temperament but not as overwrought as the first group (about 15 %).[2]

The third, the **Tea Party** group, is comprised mostly of people from the first two groups above. Before the Tea Party emerged, however, many of its supporters helped to elect the 2000 and 2004 right-wing administrations that violated conservative principles and started our nation's decline. They have yet to accept responsibility.

Rebelling against violations of conservative principles, the Tea Party came to life and during the 2010 midterm elections put up candidates to successfully challenge incumbents of both parties. The Tea Party is funded and supported by GOP lobbyists and Fox News.

When in their interest to do so, these three right wing groups band together and represent a powerful force.

The **Democratic Party** usually has more supporters but less money and depends more on smaller donations. Supporters are nearly 35 % of the electorate and are more diverse, ranging from the extreme left and left of center to the center and right of center. They have less party discipline than Republicans and ordinarily do not operate as one body either when in or out of power. They are more apt to favor compromise over deadlock.

Democrats favor the use of federal power to promote economic growth, make social progress, and help maintain a large and strong middle class. Educators, students, progressives, people of color and labor unions tend to favor this party.

Democrats have the same instincts as Republicans when it comes to seeking political power. The difference is Republicans excel at it. Another difference is that Democrats do not rally around their President as strongly as Republicans do.

The Independent, Americans Elect, No Labels and Occupy Wall Street Movements

The position of four non-partisan groups—Independent, Americans Elect, No Labels and Occupy Wall Street—is that our two-party system is not working. They support returning power to the people by reducing partisanship and ending big money corruption of our political system.

Independents are the swing voters. Their numbers now exceed each of the two major parties and are estimated at about 38 to 40 percent of the electorate. They shift their support from one party to the other depending on a number of factors, such as the economy and a particular party's leadership and agenda.

The Independents are the target of both parties in general elections because they determine the outcome. The more one party achieves success or undermines the other, the greater chance it has to attract Independents and win the next election.

An Independent movement has been underway for the past two decades. Its purpose is to "reform the partisan way our country practices politics." Independents strongly favor open primaries so they will not be locked out of elections nominating candidates for office.[3] The position of the Committee for a Unified Independent Party is that:

> **"The two parties determine who runs for office and who is allowed to vote in primaries. They draw legislative and Congressional boundaries to maximize party control and decrease uncertainty. They determine which bills come up for debate, and which amendments get buried. They serve as the official gatekeepers for all things political, and while for decades they could make the case that this control did not prevent progress, that is no longer the case. Our country is faced with monumental challenges, and our partisan political system is not up to the task."**

Leaders of the Independent Movement consider party politics an obstacle to innovation and progress, and they, in turn, seek non-partisan government. Their objective is to transform the whole political system by ending political parties and restructuring our political process. They consider themselves an alternative to partisan politics and partisan government.[4] A fine article explaining this position is in Appendix VIII.

The **Americans Elect Party** is a non-partisan movement that is being developed on the Internet. Its mission is to put country before party and American interest before special interest. Its plan is to give voters across 50 states an opportunity to nominate a presidential ticket during an Internet convention in June 2012.

No Labels is a group of Republicans, Democrats and Independents dedicated to making Washington work. They seek to represent the silent majority and end the political games and pettiness that drive the decision-making process in government.

The **Occupy Wall Street Movement** is challenging the allocation of economic and political power in this country. It wants to return power to the people. Its grievances include income inequality, money in politics and an unfair tax policy. Although non-partisan, its supporters are more apt to be independents and Democrats. The right-wing of the Republican Party opposes this movement.

A 99 % Working Group plans a nationwide election of delegates to attend a National General Assembly convening in Philadelphia on July 4, 2012. The delegates include one man and one woman from each of 435 congressional districts and Washington D.C. and one delegate from each U.S. territory. During the conference they will deliberate and create a Petition for the Redress of Grievances to be served upon the federal government before the November elections.

After the petition is ratified and served, the delegates will demand a public pledge from all elected officials to redress the grievances upon taking office. Over a dozen occupy candidates are running for office in the 2012 elections.

If our political system was working the way it should, obviously there would not be a Tea Party, or an Independent Party Movement, or an Americans Elect Party, or an Occupy Wall Street Movement, or a No Labels Movement.

Disappearance of Republican Moderates

As noted earlier, the right wing favors closed primaries when choosing its nominees for office. Independents are barred from participating.

Thus, there is less chance of nominating someone who is a moderate or representative of the district as a whole.

In earlier times, moderate statesmen of both parties in Congress supported important decisions by the President or provided constructive alternatives to those they questioned. These moderate statesmen have for the most part vanished from the Republican Party. According to researchers at the *National Journal*, more than half of the Republican Senators in 1982 were moderate, half that many in 1994, and almost none today.

Great Republican moderates of the past advanced our country in many ways and were the loyal opposition when it really counted. They had serious and honest debates and could be depended on in times of crisis. They put country first before party.

These moderate Senators included such famous ones as George Aiken, Howard Baker, Edward Brooke, William Cohen, John Sherman Cooper, Everett Dirksen, Bob Dole, Chuck Hagel, Philip Hart, Jacob Javits, Charles Mathis, Charles Percy, Margaret Chase Smith, and Arthur Vandenberg. Two have Senate office buildings named after them.

To illustrate, Republican Senator Vandenberg fought against his own party's isolationism leading up to World War II and participated in establishing the Marshall Plan to put Europe back on its feet. Senator Margaret Chase Smith challenged McCarthyism openly on the Senate floor although Senator McCarthy was a member of her own party. Not even U.S. President Dwight Eisenhower dared to challenge Senator McCarthy.

Republican moderates really cared about governing and working together to advance our country. They took a broader view that they must be team players in times of national crisis, that America comes first, and that in hard times they must be compassionate toward their struggling constituents. They believe an elected official's first obligation is to see that America succeeds. Political loyalties come second.[5] All this has changed.

Recently retired moderate Republican Senator George Voinovich challenged the direction of his own party. Prior to serving two terms in the Senate he saved Cleveland from default as mayor and then made Ohio number one as governor. During a Senate retirement speech in 2010, he admonished his own party to follow a more constructive approach.

He warned that otherwise we diminish our President in the eyes of the world; we damage his credibility on foreign policy and lessen our own national security. After retirement he said his party's attitude is, "We're going to get what we want or the country can go to hell."[5a]

A great moderate for two decades, Senator Olympia Snowe, has decided not to run for Senate in 2012 due to increasing partisanship (See her Washington Post article in Appendix IX). She says our founders wanted the Senate to operate on consensus and now we have a parallel universe: the two sides do not even talk to each other:

"I do not believe that, in the near term, the Senate can correct itself from within. It is by nature a political entity and, therefore, there must be a benefit to working across the aisle.

"As I enter a new chapter, I see a vital need for the political center in order for our democracy to flourish and to find solutions that unite us rather than divide us. It is time for a change in the way we govern ... we must return to an era of civility in government driven by a common purpose to fulfill the promise that is unique to America."

Republican moderate Senator Susan Collins joined Senator Snowe in opposition to her party with another 2012 article in the *Washington Post* entitled "Yes, the Political Center Can Be Saved" (See appendix X).

Political Conspiracies Undermining Democracy

Right-wing leadership left the current President on the perilous edge of a national emergency—huge deficits, two seemingly never ending wars, an unacceptable foreign policy, job losses in the millions, a rapidly declining stock market, and unattended, but urgent, domestic needs. (See chapters three through five).

The responsible thing for right-wing leaders to do at that time was to work constructively with the new President at recovery. Instead, they blocked the President at every turn and sought to immediately regain the power they had *just* lost. The right wing is very adept at passing on their sins to a new president and then charging him with the responsibility for them. The long-term deficits it structured into future budgets and high unemployment are but two examples (See chapter six).

When the right-wing wages continuous warfare after losing an election, the next administration has little opportunity to govern. Real progress is limited due to a partial governing body in Congress constantly being obstructed by the other body. The American people deserve better. We do not send representatives to Washington to out maneuver the people's elected president, but rather to do things that will improve our daily lives, especially in times of national crisis.

One of several ways the right wing uses to undermine our political system is a powerful misdirection machine that preys on the uninformed. A national columnist described it this way:

> **"We should not accept stories made up about our current predicament that absolve the people who put us there. We need to place the blame where it belongs in order to learn from the current crisis. Otherwise, the same people will do even more damage in the years ahead."**

Another way the right wing uses to undermine democracy is political conspiracies. The most famous one was the break-in of the Democratic National Committee headquarters at the Watergate Hotel in Washington D.C. That plot backfired and cost Nixon his presidency. Despite this severe setback, the right wing has continued to plot ways to preserve power at the nation's expense and has succeeded in three recent instances.

1. Conspiracy to retake Government in year 2000.

(a) Conducted groundless investigations of President Clinton and the First Lady and left these investigations open until the end of his two administrations.

(b) Manipulated the U.S. judiciary system by bringing a baseless sexual harassment suit against a sitting president, set up a perjury trap, got a conflict of interest investigation authorized and railroaded an unconstitutional impeachment in a lame duck House session—using blackmail to get the necessary votes (See chapter 1).

2. Conspiracy to insure a Bush second term

(a) Covered up a breach of national security at the highest level of government in face of repeated and powerful warnings of the upcoming 9/11 attacks (See chapter 2).

(b) Made unsubstantiated charges against a decorated Democratic presidential nominee's combat war record (swiftboating). In contrast, the Republican nominee had for several years evaded serving in the same war.

3. Conspiracy to reject the people's choice of president

(a) Obstructed President Obama's recovery agenda and stalled efforts to jump start the economy (See chapter 6).

(b) Permitted unnamed corporate and big money interests to begin buying elections in 2010 and 2012 (See chapter 7).

(c) Instituted anti-voting legislation in Republican-controlled states to suppress Democratic turnout (See below).

Voting is fundamental to the pursuit of freedom and equal opportunity. Historically, the right wing has attempted to remain in power by raising the specter of voter fraud and restricting voting rights of Americans. Legislation limiting access to the ballot box is a central part of the right wing agenda for the upcoming 2012 elections. This legislation is an attack on our democracy.

The idea is to reduce the number of Democrats who can vote by imposing cumbersome voting requirements. Targets are the elderly, the disabled, people of color, low-income people, students, and the homeless. A long-time brain trust and "father" of the right-wing movement, Paul Weyrick, confessed:

"As a matter of fact, I don't want everybody to vote. Our leverage in the election quite candidly goes up as the voting populace goes down."

This strategy is being promoted in a systematic campaign orchestrated by the American Legislative Exchange Council (ALEX) and funded in part by the billionaire Koch brothers who bankrolled the Tea Party. Well over thirty states are involved in an attempt to impede voters at every step of the electoral process. [6]

Voter turnout in America is already low and far less than other advanced democracies. The bills introduced and laws enacted in Republican controlled states are designed to shrink the electorate even more. Their real purpose is to turn away from the polls people who are more likely to vote Democratic.

These new restrictions suppress voting rights by curtailing early and absentee voting, restricting voter registration drives, banning same day registration, and requiring certified birth certificates and narrowly defined state photo identifications. Some bills have even precluded registration assistance at the polls.

The voting rights of some twenty-five million Americans across the nation are at stake. An overview of the voting changes already enacted for 2012 has been published by the non-partisan Brennan Center For Justice. The new restrictions affect women more than men because of changes in their names due to marriage and changes in their addresses due to separation, divorce and domestic abuse.

As always, the right wing rationale for these restrictions is voter fraud. In Ohio, a bill's sponsor was asked to produce evidence of fraud, but could not. A major probe by the Justice Department between 2002 and 2007 failed to prosecute a single person for going to the polls and impersonating an eligible voter.

The penalties are severe—years in jail and a large fine. The Brennan Center for Justice reported in 2007 that this type of fraud is incredibly difficult and fraught with risk:

"To steal even one vote by impersonation requires the impersonator to go to a precinct where he will not be recognized and the registered voter he intends to impersonate will not be recognized. The impersonator has to know that the registered voter has not already voted either in person or by absentee..."

One Ohio newspaper called a new photo restriction bill "the 21st century equivalent of a poll tax." In total, about twenty-one million people of the electorate don't have updated, state-issued photo IDs. Most Departments of Motor Vehicles (DMVs) simply require that people show some household bill to establish place of residence.

Under the Ohio bill, IDs issued by state colleges to their students do not qualify. In Wisconsin, a quarter of a million students may not be able to vote in 2012 because of cumbersome new voting requirements that no college and university can meet.[7] In essence, the right wing is discouraging student participation in their very first encounter with our democracy.

A Texas law, one of the most restrictive in the country, was promoted by Republican Governor Perry as an "emergency item." It even prohibits veterans from using their ID cards. Six activist groups have asked the Justice Department to review the Texas law. A former Texas Republican Political Director says his party's rationale of fraud is "a lie, not true and does not exist."[8]

In Indiana, photo ID laws have forced election workers to turn nuns and college students away from the polls.[9] A Supreme Court decision supporting this law noted that, while it was aimed at preventing "in person voter impersonation", the record contained no evidence of any such fraud actually occurring in Indiana at any time in its history. [9a]

Early voting has become increasingly popular. Limiting days for early voting, and on Sundays before Election Day, presents a particular problem to African Americans because they like to vote at these times.

Taxpayers will have to bear the cost of these new measures that will help the right wing win the next presidential election. For example, North Carolina will have to spend more than $20 million to educate their voters on the new requirements and provide IDs to those without them.

Getting IDs, however, will not be easy. In Wisconsin, for example, DMV offices for driver licenses are being closed in Democratic-leaning areas while others are open for only limited hours. Wisconsin also reduced the number of polling places. Many people lacking transportation, having disabilities, or being home-bound will have difficulty voting ***even if they are well known to their voting precinct***. A Wisconsin judge has since declared the law as unconstitutional.

The South Carolina Democratic Chairman referred to his state's new law as "electoral genocide." He says it is disenfranchising huge groups of people who don't have the money to go get an ID card. There are 82,000 registered voters there who lack DMV-issued identification.

In Florida the Republican governor has reversed the policy of restoring voting rights to tax-paying citizens with past felony convictions. As a result, an estimated 100,000 Floridians will not be able to vote in 2012.

The federal voting rights act prohibits discriminatory voting practices and imposing any voting qualification or prerequisite to voting that deny the right of any citizen to vote on account of race or color.

The Department of Justice has the authority to reject changes to laws of southern states that historically have imposed such discriminatory requirements. In December 2011, the Justice Department rejected the South Carolina law as discriminatory and did the same in March 2012 for the Texas law.

In a few cases, a citizen's veto campaign is underway in an attempt to undo the changes to voting rights. In Ohio, more than 318,000 citizen signatures blocked the new barriers to voting. However, the more important issue is the constitutionality of suppressing voting rights and whether our democracy is being undermined by a party obsessed with gaining power at any costs. [10]

All this effort to erect barriers to voting and intimidate voters is not new. The Bush White House, assisted by Karl Rove, fired seven reputable US attorneys on the grounds they failed to pursue charges of voter fraud in states important to Republicans. The Justice Department inspector general later said that the firings of the US attorneys were "fundamentally flawed" and raised real doubts about prosecution decisions.

Some people contend that "the only fraud in voter fraud is the allegation of fraud itself." As one observer noted, "the real problem in American elections is not the myth of voter fraud, but how few people actually participate."

More than one fourth of eligible Americans are unregistered to vote, and with new restrictions on voter registration drives, this situation can only get worse. For example, compared with the same period in 2008, 81000 fewer Floridians are registered to vote.

The way to correct this is through *universal voter registration*. It automatically registers any citizen with data in official government records; keeps the data up to date with changes in voters' names and addresses; and provides a means to correct voter registration errors at the polls on Election Day.[10a]

Advanced democracies, like Australia and New Zealand, have compulsory voting. They require their citizens to vote or pay a fine. Considering similar action here in the U.S. would further increase voter turnout and deter voter suppression.

In Republican controlled states, the right wing also opposes open primaries. This means independents, a large part of the electorate, have become second class citizens in the all important nomination process. It also means that those nominated for office will likely be less representative of their district as a whole and more extreme in their thinking.

Republican Opposition to Their Own Party

Having lost faith in his own party, a long-term GOP professional staffer (who served nearly three decades in the House and Senate) decided to retire from Congress in 2011. He says that, while Democrats have their share of problems, nothing quite matches the modern GOP. [11] Among his many observations is that the modern GOP:

- Believes no Democratic president can conceivably be legitimate;
- Appeals to the worst instincts of its fearful and angry low-information political base;
- Has merged politics and religion and uses this as a presidential test;
- Lectures other countries about the wonders of democracy, exports democracy to the middle-east countries (at the barrel of a gun) but domestically doesn't want people to vote;
- Has adopted a prime strategy of undermining Americans' belief in their own institutions of self-government so that the party against government can come out the winner;
- Legislates as if in a war, minus the shooting;

- Is increasingly hostile to the democratic values of reason, compromise and conciliation and instead uses the principal campaign strategy of "conflict and the crushing of opposition;"
- Has a psychological predisposition toward war and militarism; and
- Is becoming less and less like a traditional party in a representative democracy and becoming more like an apocalyptic cult with lunatics. He named several currently in Congress, including a 2012 presidential candidate.

The former staffer added that future electoral success, during which the GOP unleashes major policy disasters, means twilight for both the democratic process and America's status as the world's leading power.

In a July 2011 article, another Republican (retired eight-term congressman Mickey Edwards) explains why Congress is not working as envisioned in our Constitution:

- "I have seen the United State Congress as it actually functions, not a gathering of America's chosen leaders to confront, together, the problems we face, but as competing armies – on the floor, in committees, in subcommittees – determined to dominate or destroy.
- "The current process *is* a battle between warring tribes.
- "Partisan drawing of congressional-district boundaries has hurt the democratic process, leaving elected officials dependent on, and beholden to, the party bosses who draw the districts.
- "Closed primaries allow small bands of activists to limit our choices of people to represent us in making the nation's laws.
- "Our leaders govern in a system that makes cooperation almost impossible and incivility nearly inevitable, a system in which the campaign season never ends and the struggle for party advantage trumps all other considerations.
- "With the country at war and the economy in recession, our government leaders' first thoughts have been of party advantage.

- "By thinking of the House and Senate in constitutional rather than partisan terms, we would eliminate the spectacle of legislative leaders acting as though they were either members of the president's staff or his sworn enemies.
- "The problem is not division but partisanship-advantage-seeking to win political power."

The former Republican congressman suggests a number of ways to "Turn Republicans and Democrats into Americans:" (1) break the power of partisans to keep candidates off the general-election ballot, (2) turn over the process of redrawing congressional districts to an independent group, (3) change the leadership structure of congressional committees, (4) allow members of any party to offer amendments to bills, and (5) choose committee staff solely on the basis of professional qualifications.

Conclusions and Remedies

We have reached the stage in our politics and democracy where an extreme element that controls one party is so obsessed with returning to power that it will not work with or let the other party govern.

Trying to suppress voter turnout disrespects and disregards our Constitution. Allowing unlimited money contributions from unknown, ultra rich sources can only lead to unfair elections and more income inequality in America.

People of color are becoming a larger part of our voting population and one day will be in the majority. Students worried about jobs at graduation are taking a much greater interest in our politics. The right-wing's pursuit of power by restricting the voting rights of these and other groups is a losing strategy.

Unless the right wing is held accountable, these kinds of attacks on our democracy will only continue to plague our nation. The Republican Party must become a more constructive force. Until it does so, it forfeits the right to govern.

The Republican Party needs to drop its old ideas that got us into this mess, like the government is evil and the trickle-down economic theory. The invest-and-grow economics of the Clinton administration worked well for all Americans; the trickledown economics of the two right-wing administrations that followed worked well for the wealthy.

Republicans need a new brand with new ideas and new leaders with statesman-like qualities. They need to appeal to the middle class, minorities and younger people. They need to demonstrate that they really care about growing the middle class, have sound ideas and are mature enough to govern. Wasting our time for three years with things like challenging the president's citizenship only demeans their party.

Republicans need to get their minds off the next election and focus on how to strengthen the country. As elections approach, they will have ample opportunity to take their case to the public. They need to encourage their own members to challenge the status quo, present new ideas and compromise with the other party in times of dire need.

As former President Clinton said, when politicians use conflict to achieve power they find it difficult to cooperate when governing. And, he noted that not a single country in the world has succeeded with a "militant anti-government philosophy." Our former President believes that the answer to our economic problems is a smart government that invests in our future in partnership with the private sector.

What kind of politics do Americans really want – one where the political parties in Congress refuse to agree on anything regardless of merit and misinform the public about their differences – or one where the parties work together and, when they can't, tell the public something close to the truth about their differences and offer constructive alternatives?

We have seen throughout the book how power-obsessed politics have taken us on the wrong course, shaped future events for the worse and started our nation's decline. It's time for the public to take matters into their own hands and choose representatives and national leaders who put their country first over party, who do not sacrifice our long-term future for short-term gains, and who will invest in America's future for the common good.

As private citizens, we don't have to accept the way politics have been conducted over the past two decades. We have the power to change things for the future. We can hold political parties and individual members of Congress accountable and improve the caliber of leadership in the American system of government.

Among other things, this means showing up at elections. A reinvigorated American electorate that votes in large numbers can accomplish wonders. An informed public that exercises its right to vote regularly can hold politicians accountable for being overly partisan and unprofessional in their political discourse.

As long as politicians continue to be indebted to big money interests for winning elections, it will be impossible to achieve the full democracy promised to us by our founders.[12] Electoral reform will give ordinary Americans much more say in who best represents them in governing (See chapter seven).

One astute journalist said that one way to counter organized money is with organized people. Ordinary Americans are becoming increasingly empowered by the Internet which has permitted a hundred million or more people to contribute small amounts of money and time to candidates of their choice.

Campaign seasons are becoming increasing longer with each presidential election and campaign expenditures are going through the roof. Both should have their limits so that elected officials can get some work done and elected offices are not sold to the highest bidder.

Campaign expenditures can be limited based on the worth of the individual candidate to his or her particular electorate. Each willing donor would have a cap to be matched with public financing. The more small donors a candidate can attract to the campaign the greater will be the available campaign financing. In this way, taxpayers would invest in and own a piece of our democracy and, at the same time, remove the widespread corruptive influence of private big money interests.

With the public's immense voting power, political parties and candidates can be penalized and rewarded according to their performance, agenda, political behavior and respect for our institutions of democracy.

The penalty would be for voters to leave obstructionist parties in the minority and reject members of Congress who perpetually campaign, govern as partisans and use divisive tactics. The reward would be to support political parties with good leadership, a sound agenda, integrity and willingness to compromise for the public good.

Once voting results are fully analyzed under this kind of reward and penalty system and made public by the media, we will begin to see a more acceptable level of political discourse, a more unified country, and a government that works for the American people, not for politicians.

Also, Congress must reorganize itself and strengthen our electoral system by drawing from recommendations of the eight-term Republican congressman cited earlier and from those of others who have served or are now serving in Congress. Their objectives would be to:

- Substantially reduce the level of partisanship in American politics and restore a working relationship among elected officials and their leaders,
- Return the filibuster to its original intent and preclude its use as a partisan weapon of mass destruction to defeat the peoples' choice of president,
- Select members of Congress and its leaders with a demonstrated skill to work across party lines and who put country first before party, and
- Adopt a modern system of universal voter registration and insure that no one's constitutional right to vote can be taken away.

If elected officials do not make these kinds of major repairs to our system of politics, the American people must take matters into their own hands and consider alternatives. They include (1) an across-the-board-rejection at the polls of defenders of the status quo, (2) electing more women in leadership positions and (3) demanding a constitutional convention to update and renew our democracy.

Revolutionary leader, founding father, and second U.S. President, John Adams said every generation must renew our democracy. Founder and two-term President Thomas Jefferson said that every constitution can expire at times because "the earth belongs always to the living generations."

A constitutional convention can be convened to reexamine how well our democracy is working and consider the best features of other advanced democracies. These basic tenets of democracy should be at the heart of any renewed system of government:

- Take into account the interest of all persons contributing to our society,
- Allow no person or group of persons with rights guaranteed under the Constitution to be ignored or exploited by the rest of society,
- Elect lawmakers and national leaders in an open and competitive system that is easily accessible to all eligible voters,
- Permit each person's vote to be equal in weight and not be diminished by the corruptive influence of big money interests,
- Allow no branch of government to usurp the powers of others or undermine decisions of the governing majority lawfully made in accordance with the Constitution.
- Have the capacity to act and make timely decisions in meeting pressing public needs.
- Hold policymakers and lawmakers accountable for promoting the common good of the nation.
- Provide for our fourth estate, the media, to keep the public fully informed on how well our system of government is working.

"Even If Washington leads the nation in incivility, it is not likely to change until those outside of Washington demand it. What gets rewarded gets done, and for those of us in Congress, reelection is the ultimate reward. Vote out of office – or not elect in the first place – those who put partisanship over progress..."

Senator Susan Collin
"A Moderate Republican"
Washington Post, Oct 10, 2010

End Notes

1. A bleak look at America's future, David Ignatius, Washington Post, Dec. 9, 2011.

1a. "The GOP is blowing it. Brent Budowsky," *The Hill*, June 21, 2010.

2. "State of the Union: A Status Report on the Far Right," Sara Robinson, *Cognitive Policy Works*, Feb. 2, 2010.

3. "How Obama Can Be a Non-Partisan President", Jacqueline Salit, Campaign Commentary, July 13, 2011. "Open Primary Unconstitutional", Todd Dvorak, Associated Press The Coeur D'Alene Press, March 3, 2011.

4. Statement Read by Joyce Dattner, Chair of *Independent Voice. Org,* before the California leadership in Sacramento on passage of Proposition 14, June 9, 2010.

5. "An old-school trick: Put country first," David Ignatius, *Washington Post*, Sept. 16, 2010.

5a. "How the GOP Became the Party of the Rich", Tim Dickinson, Rolling Stone, Nov. 24, 2011.

6. "The GOP War on Voting, Ari Berman, Rolling Stone, August 31, 2011. "The Myth of Voter Fraud", New York Times editorial, Oct. 10, 2011.

7. "Ohio House Passes 'Nation's Most Restrictive' ID Law That Would Curb Rights of Almost 900,000 Ohioans," Tanya Somanader, *Think Progress*, March 24, 2011. "They Want to Make Voting Harder?" New York Time editorial, June 6, 2011. "How states are rigging the 2012 election" E.J. Dionne, Wash Post, June 19, 2011.

8. "Civil Rights Groups Ask DOJ To Stop Texas Voter ID law That Would Disenfranchise Students, Veterans, And The Poor", Tanya Somanader, thinkprogress.org. Sept 16, 2011.

9. "Fair Elections Block The Vote," Assault On Voting Rights, *Think Progress*, April 15, 2001. "SC voter ID law hits black precincts", Jim Davenport, The Associated Press, Oct. 19, 2011.

9a. "Voting in Plain Sight", Linda Greenhouse, New York Times, Jan. 11, 2012.

10. "Information Ahead of Senate Hearings on State Voting Legislation Threatening Voting Rights in 2011", Press Releases, Brennan Center For Justice, Sept. 9, 2011. "Statement for Congressional Forum: Excluded from Democracy: The Impact of Recent State Voting Changes", Lawrence Norden, Brennan Center For Justice, Nov. 14, 2011.

10a. "A vote for universal registration", Katrina vanden Heuvel, Washinton Post, April 23, 2012.

11. "Goodbye to All That: Reflections of a GOP Operative Who Left the Cult", Mike Lofgren, truthout.org, Sept. 3, 2011. "Congress' dysfunction long in the making", CBS News, Oct.1, 2011.

12. "Election 2010 to shatter Spending Records as Republicans Benefit from Late Cash Surge," Open Secrets Blog, Oct. 27, 2010. "Outside Spending Surges in 2010," Left and Right News, Nov. 28, 2010.

President John F. Kennedy—
A Final Comment

Over the past two decades, right-wing leaders have taken extreme measures to gain control of government and great latitude with the truth.

The right-wing obsession with power has led to **political** assassinations of two Presidents, Clinton (chapter one) and Obama (chapter six). The second political assassination enflamed right-wing supporters with false rhetoric and provoked numerous threats on the lives of members of Congress and the President.

Political and *actual* assassinations have something in common. One attempts to kill the inner life or soul and the other the human body. A number of our national leaders have been unmercifully killed when they still had much left to give the country, as in the case of President John F. Kennedy.

In an article by Frank Rich in the New York Media, he points out some similarities between Kennedy and Obama – both becoming Presidents by breaking down the barriers of religion and race, giving great speeches, being progressive centrists and having to contend with right-wing hate that engulfed both of their presidencies.

At the very inception of his presidency, President Kennedy was not fully informed on the impending CIA led invasion of Cuba at the Bay of Pigs. When he was, he refused to provide air support, fired the CIA Director and took full responsibility for the disaster.

A little more than a year later, President Kennedy had to confront Russian missiles installed in Cuba. There were enormous implications of having nearby missiles pointed directly at the United States. Our military and the CIA pressured the President for a military solution. We were on the verge of a nuclear war and the planet was in danger of becoming a nuclear wasteland.

Kennedy ignored the reckless recommendations of the Joint Chiefs of Staff and found a way to resolve the matter peacefully, and the missiles were withdrawn. According to Chairman Khrushchev's biography, had the U.S. attacked Cuba, most people in New York City would have died or been severely injured.

Afterwards, President Kennedy and Chairman Khrushchev of the Soviet Union had extensive personal correspondence on how to end the cold war and the then slowly escalating war in Vietnam.

If there is any doubt about President's Kennedy's intentions at that time, it can easily be confirmed by reading his Commencement Address at American University on June 10, 1963. It focused entirely on changing the cold war attitude and searching for peace. Five months later he was assassinated. During the remaining months of his life, President Kennedy:

- Forced a southern university to allow entry of the first African American.
- Made epic addresses on civil and voting rights, and on nuclear arms control.
- Negotiated a treaty outlawing nuclear tests on land, underwater and in space.
- Made his famous speech to over one million beleaguered and walled-off West Berliners.

He wanted peace not merely in our time, but for all time. He called on the Soviet Union to join the U.S. to prove that peace is possible. He correctly observed that the people inhabiting the U.S. and Soviet Union are not that different in their needs and dreams.

These changes in President Kennedy's foreign policy, and his earlier response to the Bay of Pigs debacle, earned President Kennedy secret distrust and hatred among the right wing hard-liners. However, they had to contend with Kennedy's worldwide popularity which almost assured his reelection.

In the 2008 book, *JFK and the Unspeakable: Why He Died and Why It Matters*, James W. Douglass floats a new conspiracy theory about Kennedy's assassination. With some Kennedy friends and family support, he suggests that right-wing elements of the military and CIA were responsible.

Douglass argues that the conspirators made the brilliant move of selecting a left-wing person, Lee Harvey Oswald, to do the deed. Oswald had returned from a stay in Russia and the CIA/FBI people monitoring his every move knew he was unstable and discontented with both communism and capitalism.

Although no hard evidence exists in the public domain to support this theory, the right wing's win-at-any-cost politics suggest that it is at least a possibility.

In our history, we've had far too many attempted and actual assassinations of our national leaders. Future leaders will continue to be in jeopardy as long as an opposition party uses a do-or-die mode of politics and enflames their supporters with false rhetoric. Out of respect for our future national leaders, we should return to a more civil discourse in our politics.

One wonders how different America would be today if John Kennedy had served two terms as President. On this point, Director Oliver Stone commented that:

> **"The murder of President Kennedy was a seminal event for me and for millions of Americans. It changed the course of history. It was a crushing blow to our country and to millions of people around the world To a large extent, the fate of our country and the future of the planet continue to be controlled by the shadowy forces of what Douglass calls "the Unspeakable." Only by unmasking these forces and confronting the truth can we restore the promise of democracy and lay claim to Kennedy's vision of peace."**

Appendix I

———•·•———

U.S. DIPLOMAT'S LETTER OF RESIGNATION

Rep. Hon. Fortney Pete Stark of California read this letter into the Congressional Record (Extensions) (Page E363-E364) on March 4, 2003.

The following is the text of John Brady Kiesling's letter of resignation to Secretary of State Colin L. Powell. Mr. Kiesling is a career diplomat who has served in United States embassies from Tel Aviv to Casablanca to Yerevan.

Dear Mr. Secretary:

I am writing you to submit my resignation from the Foreign Service of the United States and from my position as Political Counselor in U.S. Embassy Athens, effective March 7. I do so with a heavy heart. The baggage of my upbringing included a felt obligation to give something back to my country. Service as a U.S. diplomat was a dream job. I was paid to understand foreign languages and cultures, to seek out diplomats, politicians, scholars and journalists, and to persuade them that U.S. interests and theirs fundamentally coincided. My faith in my country and its values was the most powerful weapon in my diplomatic arsenal.

It is inevitable that during twenty years with the State Department I would become more sophisticated and cynical about the narrow and selfish bureaucratic motives that sometimes shaped our policies. Human nature is what it is, and I was rewarded and promoted for understanding human nature. But until this Administration it had been possible to believe that by upholding the policies of my president I was also upholding the interests of the American people and the world. I believe it no longer.

The policies we are now asked to advance are incompatible not only with American values but also with American interests. Our fervent pursuit of war with Iraq is driving us to squander the international legitimacy that has been America's most potent weapon of both offense and defense since the days of Woodrow Wilson. We have begun to dismantle the largest and most effective web of international relationships the world has ever known. Our current course will bring instability and danger, not security.

The sacrifice of global interests to domestic politics and to bureaucratic self-interest is nothing new, and it is certainly not a uniquely American problem. Still, we have not seen such systematic distortion of intelligence, such systematic manipulation of American opinion, since the war in Vietnam. The September 11 tragedy left us stronger than before, rallying around us a vast international coalition to cooperate for the first time in a systematic way against the threat of terrorism. But rather than take credit for those successes and build on them, this Administration has chosen to make terrorism a domestic political tool, enlisting a scattered and largely defeated Al Qaeda as its bureaucratic ally. We spread disproportionate terror and confusion in the public mind, arbitrarily linking the unrelated problems of terrorism and Iraq. The result, and perhaps the motive, is to justify a vast misallocation of shrinking public wealth to the military and to weaken the safeguards that protect American citizens from the heavy hand of government. September 11 did not do as much damage to the fabric of American society as we seem determined to [do] to ourselves. Is the Russia of the late Romanovs really our model, a selfish, superstitious empire thrashing toward self-destruction in the name of a doomed status quo?

We should ask ourselves why we have failed to persuade more of the world that a war with Iraq is necessary. We have over the past two years done too much to assert to our world partners that narrow and mercenary U.S. interests override the cherished values of our partners. Even where our aims were not in question, our consistency is at issue. The model of Afghanistan is little comfort to allies wondering on what basis we plan to rebuild the Middle East, and in whose image and interests. Have we indeed become blind, as Russia is blind in Chechnya, as Israel is blind in the Occupied Territories, to our own advice, that overwhelming military power is not the answer to terrorism? After the shambles of post-war Iraq joins the shambles in Grozny and Ramallah, it will be a brave foreigner who forms ranks with Micronesia to follow where we lead.

We have a coalition still, a good one. The loyalty of many of our friends is impressive, a tribute to American moral capital built up over a century. But our closest allies are persuaded less that war is justified than that it would be perilous to allow the U.S. to drift into complete solipsism. Loyalty should be reciprocal. Why does our President condone the swaggering and contemptuous approach to our friends and allies this Administration is fostering, including among its most senior officials. Has "oderint dum metuant" really become our motto?

I urge you to listen to America's friends around the world. Even here in Greece, purported hotbed of European anti-Americanism, we have more and closer friends than the American newspaper reader can possibly imagine. Even when they complain about American arrogance, Greeks know that the world is a difficult and dangerous place, and they want a strong international system, with the U.S. and EU in close partnership. When our friends are afraid of us rather than for us, it is time to worry. And now they are afraid. Who will tell them convincingly that the United States is as it was, a beacon of liberty, security, and justice for the planet?

Mr. Secretary, I have enormous respect for your character and ability. You have preserved more international credibility for us than our policy deserves, and salvaged something positive from the excesses of an ideological and self-serving Administration. But your loyalty to the President goes too far. We are straining beyond its limits an international system we built with such toil and treasure, a web of laws, treaties, organizations, and shared values that sets limits on our foes far more effectively than it ever constrained America's ability to defend its interests.

I am resigning because I have tried and failed to reconcile my conscience with my ability to represent the current U.S. Administration. I have confidence that our democratic process is ultimately self-correcting, and hope that in a small way I can contribute from outside to shaping policies that better serve the security and prosperity of the American people and the world we share.

Appendix II

ARTICLE BY REV. DR. GRAHAM STANDISH:
A COUNTRY DIVIDED BY CHRIST

Post-gazette.com June 12, 2005.

If you are a Christian, how should you vote, Republican or Democrat? As a seminary student in the 1980s, the choice seemed clear, at least for many of my classmates. We could not be Christian and Republican. We especially could not be Christian and vote for Ronald Reagan. The only choice was to be a Democrat. You can imagine that I felt a bit odd being a registered Republican who happened to vote for Ronald Reagan...twice. Apparently I wasn't much of a Christian back then.

How time changes everything. Today, Christians all over the country, in print and on conservative talk radio, suggest that the only political option for Christians is to be Republican. During the last election, churches nationwide urged their members, and Christians their friends, to vote for George W. Bush. They simultaneously attacked John Kerry's faith, suggesting that he should be barred from Roman Catholic communion because of his political beliefs. Apparently, to be a Christian now means to be a Republican.

Ironically, I left the Republican Party in 1992 and registered as an independent precisely because I sensed the Republican Party slipping away from the Christianity to which I had committed my life. Why? Among other things, I could no longer abide the Republican-sanctioned, Lee Atwater orchestrated style of politics in which politicians attack, denigrate, eviscerate and even falsely accuse each other. This was a style of politics that became a mainstay of the 1988 elections and remains a staple of politics today. It skirts the issues in favor of assailing the character of the enemy.

This attack-and-accuse style of politics has grown fiercer over the years, yet it conflicts with a Christian Gospel that says "love your enemies, bless those who curse you, do good to those who hate you and pray for those who persecute you," and to "be completely humble and gentle; be patient, bearing one another in love."

For a time I considered joining the Democratic Party, but they seemed to have little interest in people of faith, and my leanings are still more Republican than Democrat. I still share many of the Republican economic and social beliefs, but I'm left in a quandary, and I'm not alone.

There are millions of Christians who lean Republican, but have found that the Christianity of the Republican Party is a strand of Christianity that promotes a narrow Gospel, while ignoring much of what Christianity has always taught about caring for the poor, the virtues of sacrificing self for the welfare of others, and the need for humility, compassion and peace. Too many Republican Party leaders have aligned themselves with a fundamentalist brand of Protestant Christianity characterized by black-and white, us-versus-them perspectives: we're saved, you're not; we're right, you're wrong; we conservatives are right and virtuous, you liberals are wrong and sinful.

This kind of thinking bleeds into their political rhetoric as they assert a kind of divine mandate for proposed programs and platforms. The Republican Party has been guided in this way of politicking by fundamentalists like Jerry Falwell, Pat Robertson, Ralph Reed, Rick Scarborough of the Patriot Pastors Network and James Dobson of Focus on the Family, among others, who have an agenda to make the United States a so-called "Christian" nation, with little room for Christians like me with different perspectives. Many of them call themselves evangelicals, despite the fact that the evangelical viewpoint actually is much broader and allows for much more diversity of opinion and belief.

Fundamentalism isn't restricted to American politics. Religious fundamentalism has a grip on much of the world. We are in an international struggle against fundamentalist Muslim terrorists who want to create truly "Muslim" nations to counteract a modern world that has strayed too far from the Quran. Israel struggles to appease Jewish fundamentalists who believe that abandoning settlements in the West Bank erodes Israel's divine rights as a "Jewish" nation. Even the Roman Catholic Church is grappling with its own fundamentalists who want to return the church to its pre-Vatican II days.

Why do so many non-fundamentalist Christians follow fundamentalist agendas, especially when it comes to politics? One answer is that influential fundamentalists have learned to articulate rigid beliefs in a moderate and compelling language that softens the hardness of their position.

For example, in Kansas, fundamentalists have put their weight behind a proposal that "intelligent design" be taught in biology classes. Intelligent design is an idea that sounds very much like what the Roman Catholic Church and most mainline Protestant churches worldwide believe: that while evolution may be the mechanism of creation, God is the architect, engineer and project manager. Fundamentalists hope that the teaching of "intelligent design" in schools will take them one step closer to barring the teaching of evolution in schools. What they don't reveal is their belief that there is only one truth: their religious truth. There is little room for thinking that integrates the insights of both religion and science.

Fundamentalists have also learned to employ an issue-reduction strategy using people and their stories to oversimplify complex issues in order to promote a fundamentalist ideology.

The Terry Schiavo case was a great example of this. Fundamentalists who heavily influence the Republican Party used her to reframe the issue of euthanasia by reducing it to a portrayal of a virtuous family trying to keep a disabled (they refused to call her comatose) woman alive, while her evil husband tried to kill her. They prompted the media and Republican rhetoric with all sorts of unsubstantiated accusations that Michael Schiavo was a greedy and abusive husband who wanted to kill Terry for his own personal gain. In doing so, they reduced the larger issue of euthanasia to a simple equation they hoped all would agree with: extending life is virtuous, while euthanasia is evil.

What they didn't expect was that the majority of Americans, especially mainstream Christians, many of whom have grappled with end-of-life issues in their own families, believe that this issue is not so simple. They also never proposed an alternative Christian suggestion, one that is very much in keeping with the biblical mandate to make "every effort to maintain the unity of the Spirit in the bond of peace." What would have happened if Christians had encouraged this traumatized and divided family to seek reconciliation and to prayerfully discern an answer together? What if Republican politicians had united all of us behind this kind of solution rather than reducing the issue to a divisive one of good versus evil?

This current mixture of Christianity and politics is troublesome because the more religion identifies with a particular political movement, the more that movement erodes religion. Politics, by its very nature, is a realm that is often tainted by pride and a desire for power that can bring out the worst in humans because the pursuit of power corrupts. It's for this reason that Jesus said we should render unto Caesar that which is Ceasar's, and render unto God that which is God's. Mixing politics and religion causes too many people to confuse Caesar's empire with God's kingdom.

Religion does have a place in political discourse, yet Christians need to be sure they don't confuse a politically expedient position with God's position. God's position is often unclear, especially in many of the gray areas of life. Presenting one political party as "the Christian party" is particularly troublesome because distilling religious faith down to political terms drains religion of its ability to lead people to move beyond a politics of self-interest.

Party affiliation doesn't make a person a Christian. There are millions of Christians who serve Christ faithfully as members of both major political parties; for each party represents particular concerns of Christianity, but neither captures them entirely. The Republicans are not the Christian party, even if millions of Christians are Republicans.

I believe that those of us who are Christian and take politics seriously need to resist the tendency to align our beliefs to strongly with any particular political movement.

Christians need to find a way to take the Gospel seriously, while simultaneously avoiding the assumption that one political party can embody the concerns of our faith. And if we are true to our faith, we need to embrace a political stance that expects politicians to seek solutions in line with our beliefs, and in a way that seeks unity rather than division.

Perhaps it is time to expect more from Republican and Democratic politicians, demanding that if they proclaim a Christian mantle, they begin acting with Christian regard for others, even their enemies, even each other.

Appendix III

JOHN MCCAIN IN CRISIS

A BUZZFLASH GUEST CONTRIBUTION Oct. 29, 2008
by Burt Hall

Presidential candidate John McCain's response to 9/11 showed Americans all they need to know about his "crisis management" abilities and foreign policy judgment. Early on, McCain embraced false intelligence and advocated blaming Iraq for al- Qaeda's terrorist attacks on the United States.

Soon after the 9/11 catastrophe, McCain announced that Iraq would be the "second phase" of the war on terror – adding that it might even be the source of our anthrax attacks at the U.S. Capitol.

In December 2001, McCain joined a few Senators in a letter to the White House saying Saddam had to be removed from power because there was "no doubt" that he intended to use weapons of mass destruction against the United States and its allies. In January 2002, aboard the aircraft carrier Theodore Roosevelt, McCain told sailors and airmen: "Next up, Baghdad!" He repeated these thoughts on CNN.

Then, in February 2002, McCain made a major speech at an international conference in Munich urging that we target rogue regimes and asking Europeans to join us. Iraq was at the top of McCain's list. He said Iraq had weapons of mass destruction, terrorist training grounds and a relationship with al-Qaeda. Eventually, he linked Saddam to international terrorists, the 9/11 attacks and assured us that the "Iraqi people will greet us as liberators" and "we will win easily."

In short, McCain was making a case for war six months before the administration did publicly. Over the next year, he went on to sell the war to the public and Congress and co-chair a committee on liberation of Iraq. This was our first look at how McCain would react to a crisis.

After much similar rhetoric from the administration, Congress authorized in October 2002 possible use of force in Iraq. Congress specified, however, that the President support existing UN Security Council resolutions and use "diplomatic or other peaceful means" where feasible.

In accordance with UN resolutions, international inspectors returned to find out the truth about Iraq's weapons. The UN sent in 250 experts from 60 countries. Eventually, they enjoyed full access and made nearly 1000 inspections before the U.S. invasion.

In January 2003, two months before the invasion, the Chief of nuclear inspections (Nobel Prize winner Dr. ElBaradei of the International Atomic Energy Agency) began reporting findings on his inspections to the UN Security Council. He raised doubts that a nuclear program actually existed in Iraq. Then, on March 7, 2003, he reported no findings of a nuclear program.

He also found that U.S. intelligence on an Iraq procurement of uranium from Niger was based on a fake document, and that U.S. intelligence on Iraq's aluminum tubes for enriching uranium was unfounded. No illegal weapons had yet been found.

At this point anyone insisting on war was doing so, not in our country's best interest, but for their own reasons. Bush ordered the invasion anyway, forcing the UN inspectors to leave for their own safety. They left on March 17/18, 2003. President Clinton said U.N. inspectors should have been allowed to finish their job.

Former presidential candidate, Bob Graham, chaired the Senate Intelligence Committee at the time and was one of the few to actually review the CIA intelligence submitted to Congress. He felt that (1) the intelligence was flimsy, (2) Iraq posed only a negligible threat, (3) we were being manipulated by the administration and (4) we would be diverting resources from the more important terrorist front in Afghanistan. He voted against the war.

As a key senator on the powerful Armed Services Committee, McCain had access to the UN inspection data and U.S. intelligence, along with Chairman Bob Graham's views on it. He was in a strong position to insist on getting the facts. Instead, McCain continued to be the war's chief proponent and even expressed impatience for the invasion. One-fourth of the Senate did not buy either McCain's or the administration's case for war and voted against it.

Some members of Congress have acknowledged their errors in authorizing the war, McCain has not. He continues to justify his position by saying foreign countries had gathered the same intelligence that we did – and he would vote for the Iraq war again.

Had McCain checked with either our CIA European chief of intelligence or the UN inspectors, he would have discovered that the key source regarding Iraq's biological weapons arsenal was an Iraqi defector in Germany called "Curveball." The defector was known to be unstable, and his information was reportedly vague, mostly secondhand and impossible to confirm. The German supervisor of intelligence said that when he heard Colin Powell's presentation at the UN he was:

"Aghast", "shocked" - "Mein Gott! We had always told them it was not proven - It was not hard intelligence."

The German government opposed the Iraq invasion. Had McCain performed his Congressional oversight role correctly, it would have been evident that U.S. intelligence was faulty, that it was then being disproved by inspectors on the ground in Iraq, and that Chairman Graham of the Senate Intelligence Committee had assessed the situation correctly.

When the war got out of control McCain blamed the administration's execution, ignoring the fact that (1) he had already praised war planners Rumsfeld and Cheney, and (2) it was his own impetuous role that led us there.

Several independent sources and Bob Woodward's new book differ with McCain on the "surge." solution to the reduced violence in Iraq. They maintain that other factors were primarily responsible for the reduced violence – (1) a Sunni decision to rebel against al-Qaeda and accept monthly U.S. cash payments to secure their neighborhoods, (2) a cease fire declared by the largest Shiite militia, and (3) the U.S. military fighting a smarter war by (a) employing new innovative measures to target and kill key insurgent leaders, and (b) protecting the population and compensating for war damages.

During the 2008 presidential campaign, al-Qaeda supported a McCain presidency on the grounds that he will be "impetuous" and "exhaust the U.S. militarily and economically" – their ultimate goal.

Appendix IV

REMEDIES TO REPAIR OUR SYSTEM OF GOVERNMENT

- **Create Constitutional standards (chp.1)**

  - Investigating a president
  - Impeaching a president

- **War Powers Act (chp. 2,3,4)**

  - President must inform public/Congress of imminent domestic terror threat
  - Public hearings with executive on alternatives to war/ occupation/exit strategy
  - If authorized, reinstitute draft temporarily, raise taxes, insure shared sacrifice

- **Foreign Policy (chp. 4)**

  - Outlaw nuclear weapons

- **Responses to international terrorism (chp. 4)**

  - Develop new policy/not wars

- **Health Care Policy (chp.5)**

    – Experiment with improvements to reform act, including single-payer system

- **Reform Tax policy (chp. 7)**

    – Simplify tax code
    – Remove loopholes, subsidies, havens
    – Increase *effective* tax rates for high income people/ corporations

- **Overhaul electoral system (chp.7 and 8)**

    – Remove big money, corporate influence
    – No secret identity for donations
    – Support partial public financing
    – Independently redraw state districts to permit competitive/representative elections
    – Adopt universal voter registration and require states to promote rather than restrict voting rights
    – Adopt compulsory voting if found useful
    – Elect presidents by popular vote

- **Reform Investigative commissions (chp. 2)**

    – Appoint members with broad expertise, not retired politicians conflicted by party loyalty
    – Require accountability at highest levels of government
    – Reopen official record on 9/11 accountability

- **Hold public hearings on media purpose, conduct in our democracy (chp. 7)**

    - Ownership, degree of independence
    - Use for political gain
    - Investigative capacity

- **Restore integrity of Supreme Court (chp. 7)**

    - Establish system of judicial ethics
    - Justices step aside on conflicts of interest
    - Limit participation in overt political activities
    - Reconsider lifetime appointments

- **Reorganize Congress (chp. 8)**

    - Establish a body to reform how Congress operates
    - Substantially reduce partisanship in American politics
    - Preclude use of the filibuster as a partisan weapon of mass obstruction
    - Select congressional leaders able to work across party lines and put country first before party

- **Educate public to reward/penalize politicians according to (chp. 8)**

    - performance, agenda, integrity, political behavior and respect for democratic institutions

Appendix V

---·•·---

PATRIOT MILLIONAIRES: LET THE BUSH
TAX CUTS EXPIRE ONCE AND FOR ALL

Tuesday 29 November 2011
by: Rose Aguilar, Truthout | News Analysis

Patriot Millionaires for Fiscal Strength, a group of citizens who make more than $1 million a year, met with politicians from both parties on Wednesday, November 16, in Washington, DC, with a unified message: Let the Bush tax cuts expire once and for all, and return the top marginal tax rate back to the Clinton-era levels.

Guy Saperstein, a former civil rights attorney and member of the Patriot Millionaires, said the most "substantive and revealing" meeting took place with supercommittee member Sen. John Kerry (D-Massachusetts). The group spent 75 minutes repeatedly and sharply telling Senator Kerry that the Bush tax cuts should expire.

"He told us a number of things that I would put in a disturbing category," says Saperstein. "We told him the Bush tax cuts should not be restored. That's our main point. He tried to sell us on the idea of reducing the top tax rates from 35 percent down to 28 percent. He tried to make the argument that it could be made up by closing loopholes elsewhere. We were astonished by that."

According to facts on the Patriot Millionaires' web site, letting tax cuts for the top 2 percent expire as scheduled would pay down the debt by $700 billion over the next ten years. In 1963, millionaires had a top marginal tax rate of 91 percent; in 1976, millionaires had a top marginal tax rate of 70 percent; today, millionaires have a top marginal tax rate of 35 percent. Between 1979 and 2007, incomes for the wealthiest 1 percent of Americans rose by 281 percent.

According to the National Priorities Project and Citizens for Tax Justice, the first decade of the Bush tax cuts, from 2001 to 2010, cost $955 billion; the Obama extension, from 2011 - 2012, cost $229 billion; the proposed extension, from 2013 to 2021, would cost $2.02 trillion; the total cost is $3.2 trillion.

Patriot Millionaires for Fiscal Strength isn't the only group of wealthy individuals calling for more progressive tax policies and an end to the Bush tax cuts.

Members of Responsible Wealth, a network of over 700 wealthy individuals who advocate for fair taxes and corporate accountability, recently sent a letter to members of the supercommittee. It says:

We support taxing capital gains and dividends at the same rate as ordinary income. We support progressive rates for the estate tax and a lower exemption. In addition, we support ensuring that large corporations pay their fair share by ending corporate tax loopholes and preventing use of offshore tax havens, and we support a financial transaction tax.

The idea that business owners and wealthy individuals will not invest unless marginal income tax rates and capital gains rates are low is a myth, and should not be used to justify further extensions of tax cuts for the wealthy. We invest when there is a profit to be made, not because tax rates on our profits are low. History shows that when marginal tax rates and capital gains rates were much higher than today, including the 1950s and 1960s and as recently as the 1990s, the economy was strong, investments were made, businesses thrived and millions of jobs were created. Furthermore, if the members of the committee fail to reach agreement, we do not believe the economy or investment levels will be harmed.

Like the majority of Americans, we believe that cutting Social Security, Medicare, Medicaid, unemployment insurance, education and research is completely unacceptable. We note that Social Security has no connection to our current deficit. We believe that a reduction in unnecessary military spending should be at least half of any spending cuts.

Because of the Occupy movement, these issues and facts are getting more media attention and the 99 percent are now in everyday conversations. So, who are the 1 percent?

The 1 percent bring in at least $350,000 a year and have at least $8 million in personal wealth, according to Christian Weller, senior fellow at the Center for American Progress, and associate professor in the department of Public Policy and Public Affairs at University of Massachusetts. On average, the 1 percent bring in $1 million a year in income and have $14 million in wealth. Approximately 1.5 million households are in the 1 percent.

In addition to raising awareness about tax policies, these groups also aim to counter the false "tax cuts create jobs" narrative we constantly hear in the national dialog.

"The main line that the other side has been pushing, and it's seductive, is that reductions in marginal tax rates lead to economic growth. If that were true, it would be a compelling argument. The problem is, it's not true," says Garrett Gruener, founder of Ask.com, co-founder of venture capital firm Alta Partners and member of the Patriotic Millionaires. "Relatively modest changes in the tax code, which have had massive effects on the budget have had no effect on entrepreneurs."

In a September 2010 Los Angeles Time op-ed called "I'm rich; tax me more," Gruener writes:

Now that the Bush tax cuts are about to expire, Republicans are again arguing that taxes should remain low for the wealthy. The idea is that this will spur people like me to put more capital to work and start more ventures, which will create new jobs, power the economy and ultimately produce more tax revenues. It's a beguiling theory, but it's one that hasn't worked before and won't work now.

Instead, Congress should let the Bush tax cuts expire for the wealthiest Americans and use the additional tax revenues that are generated to invest in infrastructure and research. "Invest" is the right word. Putting money into infrastructure - such as roads, bridges, broadband, the smart grid and public transit - as well as carefully chosen research initiatives provides a foundation for future growth. As important, it puts funds in the hands of those who will spend them, generating demand that will pull us out of our economic crisis and toward a new cycle of growth.

No one particularly enjoys paying taxes, but one lesson we should have learned by now is that for the good of the country, we need to tax people like me more. At a minimum, we need to return to the tax rates of the Clinton era, when the economy performed far better. Simply taxing the wealthiest 2% of Americans at the same rates they were taxed before the Bush tax cuts could reduce the national deficit by $700 billion over the next 10 years. Remember, paying slightly more in personal income taxes won't change my investment choices at all, and I don't think a higher tax rate will change the investment decisions of most other high earners."

Resource Generation, an organization for young people with wealth who are committed to social change, is also calling on Congress to let the Bush tax cuts expire. "We stand with the 99 percent," says Burke Stansbury, a board member of Resource Generation. Stansbury inherited a little more than $1 million dollars and is expected to inherit even more. "It's all about taxes when you talk about unequal distribution of wealth in this country. The tax system has become more and more regressive."

Resource Generation started the blog We are the 1 percent: We stand with the 99 percent. The site says, "Tax me! I support proposals to raise taxes for wealthy households like my own. No budget cuts until we raise revenue from those of us who have benefited the most and have the greatest capacity to pay."

Anti-tax crusaders like Grover Norquist and conservative outlets like The Daily Caller say that if people like Saperstein and Stansbury want to pay more taxes, they should write a check to the Department of Treasury. That's obviously missing the larger point. Watch members of the Patriotic Millionaires respond to a Daily Caller reporter's request to have them write individual checks to the Department of Treasury.

"This is not charity," said Saperstein in response. "Taxes are not charity. They're not voluntary. They're something society commits to do together." Donating to the Department of Treasury individually would "have no impact whatsoever."

Anti-tax advocates also say the government shouldn't be providing social services; leave that to nonprofits and churches. Stansbury says philanthropy isn't the solution. "A handful of people with money donating it is all well and good, but that isn't going to bring about the broad based structural change that we need in this country," he says. "That's why standing up with a political voice and speaking as people with wealth who are in favor of higher taxes on the wealthy is a powerful way to support this movement

Appendix VI

────◆•◆────

A BILLIONAIRE'S VIEWS ON TAXES

Raise Taxes on Rich to Reward True Job Creators: Nick Hanauer

It is a tenet of American economic beliefs, and an article of faith for Republicans that is seldom contested by Democrats: If taxes are raised on the rich, job creation will stop.

Trouble is, sometimes the things that we know to be true are dead wrong. For the larger part of human history, for example, people were sure that the sun circles the Earth and that we are at the center of the universe. It doesn't, and we aren't. The conventional wisdom that the rich and businesses are our nation's "job creators" is every bit as false.

I'm a very rich person. As an entrepreneur and venture capitalist, I've started or helped get off the ground dozens of companies in industries including manufacturing, retail, medical services, the Internet and software. I founded the Internet media company aQuantive Inc., which was acquired by Microsoft Corp. (MSFT) in 2007 for $6.4 billion. I was also the first non-family investor in Amazon.com Inc. (AMZN)

Even so, I've never been a "job creator." I can start a business based on a great idea, and initially hire dozens or hundreds of people. But if no one can afford to buy what I have to sell, my business will soon fail and all those jobs will evaporate.

That's why I can say with confidence that rich people don't create jobs, nor do businesses, large or small. What does lead to more employment is the feedback loop between customers and businesses. And only consumers can set in motion a virtuous cycle that allows companies to survive and thrive and business owners to hire. An ordinary middle-class consumer is far more of a job creator than I ever have been or ever will be.

Theory of Evolution

When businesspeople take credit for creating jobs, it is like squirrels taking credit for creating evolution. In fact, it's the other way around.

It is unquestionably true that without entrepreneurs and investors, you can't have a dynamic and growing capitalist economy. But it's equally true that without consumers, you can't have entrepreneurs and investors. And the more we have happy customers with lots of disposable income, the better our businesses will do.

That's why our current policies are so upside down. When the American middle class defends a tax system in which the lion's share of benefits accrues to the richest, all in the name of job creation, all that happens is that the rich get richer.

And that's what has been happening in the U.S. for the last 30 years.

Since 1980, the share of the nation's <u>income</u> for fat cats like me in the top 0.1 percent has increased a shocking 400 percent, while the share for the bottom 50 percent of Americans has declined 33 percent. At the same time, effective tax rates on the superwealthy fell to 16.6 percent in 2007, from 42 percent at the peak of U.S. productivity in the early 1960s, and about 30 percent during the expansion of the 1990s. In my case, that means that this year, I paid an 11 percent rate on an eight-figure income.

One reason this policy is so wrong-headed is that there can never be enough superrich Americans to power a great economy. The annual earnings of people like me are hundreds, if not thousands, of times greater than those of the average American, but we don't buy hundreds or thousands of times more stuff. My family owns three cars, not 3,000. I buy a few pairs of pants and a few shirts a year, just like most American men. Like everyone else, I go out to eat with friends and family only occasionally.

It's true that we do spend a lot more than the average family. Yet the one truly expensive line item in our budget is our airplane (which, by the way, was manufactured in <u>France</u> by <u>Dassault Aviation SA (AM)</u>), and those annual costs are mostly for fuel (from the <u>Middle East</u>). It's just crazy to believe that any of this is more beneficial to our economy than hiring more teachers or police officers or investing in our infrastructure.

More Shoppers Needed

I can't buy enough of anything to make up for the fact that millions of unemployed and <u>underemployed Americans</u> can't buy any new clothes or enjoy any meals out. Or to make up for the decreasing consumption of the tens of millions of middle-class families that are barely squeaking by, buried by spiraling costs and trapped by stagnant or declining wages.

If the average American family still got the same share of income they earned in 1980, they would have an astounding $13,000 more in their pockets a year. It's worth pausing to consider what our economy would be like today if middle-class consumers had that additional income to spend.

It is mathematically impossible to invest enough in our economy and our country to sustain the middle class (our customers) without <u>taxing the top 1 percent</u> at reasonable levels again. Shifting the burden from the 99 percent to the 1 percent is the surest and best way to get our consumer-based economy rolling again.

Significant tax increases on the about $1.5 trillion in collective income of those of us in the top 1 percent could create hundreds of billions of dollars to invest in our economy, rather than letting it pile up in a few bank accounts like a huge clot in our nation's economic circulatory system.

Consider, for example, that a puny 3 percent surtax on incomes above $1 million would be enough to maintain and expand the current payroll tax cut beyond December, preventing a $1,000 increase on the average worker's taxes at the worst possible time for the economy. With a few more pennies on the dollar, we could invest in rebuilding schools and infrastructure. And even if we imposed a millionaires' surtax and rolled back the Bush- era tax cuts for those at the top, the taxes on the richest Americans would still be historically low, and their incomes would still be astronomically high.

We've had it backward for the last 30 years. Rich businesspeople like me don't create jobs. Middle-class consumers do, and when they thrive,

U.S. businesses grow and profit. That's why <u>taxing the rich</u> to pay for investments that benefit all is a great deal for both the middle class and the rich.

So let's give a break to the true job creators. Let's tax the rich like we once did and use that money to spur growth by putting purchasing power back in the hands of the middle class. And let's remember that capitalists without customers are out of business.

(<u>Nick Hanauer</u> is a founder of Second Avenue Partners, a venture capital company in <u>Seattle</u> specializing in early state startups and emerging technology. He has helped launch more than 20 companies, including aQuantive Inc. and Amazon.com, and is the co-author of two books, "The True Patriot" and "The Gardens of Democracy." The opinions expressed are his own.)

To contact the writer of this article: Nick Hanauer at Nick@secondave.com.

To contact the editor responsible for this article: Max Berley at <u>mberley@bloomberg.net</u>.

Appendix VII

WHY THE CITIZENS UNITED DECISION IS CONSTITUTIONALLY FLAWED

An Excerpt From Article: "The Problem With Citizens United Is Not Corporate Personhood"

Tuesday 17 January 2012
by: Rob Hager and James Marc Leas, Truthout | News Analysis

The *Citizens United* decision is constitutionally flawed for two reasons that have nothing to do with corporate personhood. Each of these flaws provides adequate grounds for Congress to overturn not just one, but all of the Supreme Court decisions relating to private money in politics since 1976.

First, the Roberts 5 stepped outside the court's constitutional authority by taking up and deciding cases concerning election integrity. Maintaining the integrity of elections was a political question of such importance to the founding fathers who wrote the Constitution that in Article I, Sections 4 and 5, they specifically consigned to the elected Congress both regulation and judging of the manner of holding elections. The founders rightly understood that Congress would be far more subject to popular pressure to maintain election integrity than would the appointed-for-life members of the court. Taking up a case and overturning a law that provides for election integrity infringes a power specifically assigned to Congress, thereby undermining the separation of powers. This also violates the court's own well-established precedent of refusing jurisdiction concerning political questions. The court followed this traditional rule defining the boundary between judicial and legislative issues from the 1803 decision in *Marbury v. Madison* until the *Buckley* decision in 1976. Every decision widening the gates to money in politics since *Buckley*, including *Citizens United*, has violated the same constitutional principle prohibiting court jurisdiction over such political questions.

Second, even if the court had constitutional authority to take up an issue of election integrity, which it does not, the court overruled a fully supported legislative finding that private money in elections causes sufficient harm to justify its regulation, even accepting the distorted view that money in the form of electioneering expenditures is the kind of speech the First Amendment was intended to protect.

By contrast, the public has a far more profound and compelling interest in preventing the death of representative democracy by allowing continued auction of its elections and laws to wealthy corporations. Corporations profit from the government policies and government contracts they receive in exchange for their payoffs to and for politicians. For example, a study done by Raquel Alexander, Susan Scholz, and Stephen Mazza of the University of Kansas found a financial return on investment of $220 for every dollar spent on lobbying, including election-cycle lobbying. This and other evidence of corruption was found to be unimportant by the pro-corporate Roberts 5 in *Citizens United*. The court instead willfully misinterpreted the language of the First Amendment as providing such absolute right to an abstract listener to hear corporate advertisements as to overshadow the public's greater interest in preventing private money from corrupting elections and government, disenfranchising the many by the money, and causing elected politicians to divert federal and state money toward their corporate benefactors.

The sterile, highly technical issue of corporate personhood is an antiquated doctrine that played no role in *Citizens United* or any of the other election cases. From a practical point of view, as the Supreme Court itself pointed out, whether corporations should have First Amendment rights is the wrong question to ask, and, also, the wrong argument to wage. Limiting the scope of who can enjoy speech rights alienates such potential allies as the American Civil Liberties Union (ACLU) and diverts energy away from the actual constitutional problems.

A public aroused by and sympathetic to Occupy Wall Street may pressure Congress for an immediately available solution already provided in the Constitution and based on ordinary majority votes, as described in the "Constitutional Amendment Not Needed: Congress Already Has a Remedy" article. Diverting this public into seeking an unnecessary constitutional amendment on an irrelevant issue allows the serious threat to democracy created by the present Supreme Court majority to continue for the 2012 election, and on into the indefinite future.

———

While corporate advertising often works to elect candidates favorable to the corporations, it does not appear to satisfy the democratic aspirations of the public: "the latest Rasmussen Reports national telephone survey finds that just 20 percent of likely US voters say the federal government has the consent of the governed."

———

The urgency of removing private money from elections demands first properly understanding the basis for the court's decisions. It also requires determination not to be diverted by politicians, fundraising public interest organizations or professional activists from using that understanding to create an effective strategy.

Fortunately, an effective strategy does not require a constitutional amendment, whether for the irrelevant task of repealing corporate personhood or for the imperative task of excluding private money - not just for-profit corporate money - from elections.

Without the corporate personhood and constitutional amendment diversions, Sen. Sanders, Rep. Deutch and an aroused public can demand that Congress use its existing constitutional powers under Article III, Section 2 to restore the traditional limits on court jurisdiction over the political question of private money in elections. Then Congress will be free to pass legislation abolishing corrupting private finance of elections. While substantial public pressure is still needed for Congress to pass this legislation with ordinary majority votes, the barrier to success is far lower than the third-thirds vote in each house and ratification by three-fourths of the states required for a constitutional amendment. This direct route to restoring government of, by and for the people addresses the actual constitutional problems raised by the court, removes court power to find other creative vehicles to corrupt election and is available now without a constitutional amendment.

Appendix VIII

———•:•———

SPECIAL ARTICLE BY CYNTHIA CARPATHIOS: INDEPENDENT VOTERS URGE REFORMS TO LIMIT PARTISAN POLITICAL POWER

March 10, 2012 © 2012 cleveland.com.

According to a recent New York Times/CBS News poll, Americans' distrust of government is at its highest level, with 89 percent of Americans saying they distrust our government. Another 74 percent say the country is on the wrong track, and 84 percent disapprove of Congress.

It's easy to blame elected officials for the dysfunction in government. And each election cycle hope is raised that if we just elect the right person, the political gridlock that characterizes our current situation will be reversed.

But what if it's not an issue of voting in the right people? What if the parties' control over the political process is a structural problem that has made it impossible for elected officials to govern because party interests trump every other concern?

Voters are increasingly showing their lack of support for partisan politics. According to a recent Gallup poll, 40 percent of Americans identify as independents. Independents have become a permanent fixture in America's political landscape. We are a plurality of voters, but we have no representation.

I've identified as an independent most of my adult life. But in Ohio, by voting for candidates in a primary election, I automatically become a party member and can be forced to sign a loyalty oath if I want to change which party primary I vote in for the next election. If I want to remain an independent, I'm excluded from voting for candidates in primary elections altogether, though expected to fund these elections as a taxpayer. That's just one example of how party privilege trumps voter rights in this day and age.

Independents are starting to get organized and address the need for structural reforms. In Ohio, independents have formed a group called Independent Ohio and are participating in a national campaign led by IndependentVoting.org to pressure Congress for hearings on the second-class status of independents. The purpose of the hearings is to shine a spotlight on the biases independents face as a way of laying the foundation for change.

Independents want reforms that can prevent government from functioning exclusively on a partisan basis: open primaries, nonpartisan elections, nonpartisan redistricting reform, putting independents on the Federal Election Commission and reducing the domination of the parties over the people.

These reforms open up the process and empower the American people. Without structural changes to our political process, the people we elect—regardless of how much we support their program goals and no matter how committed or competent they are—will not be able to accomplish much. In a system based on self-preservation for the parties, taking care of the business of America takes a back seat. Independents are working to open up the political dialogue and transform the political landscape—so that the work of America can move ahead.

Appendix IX

———•◦•———

SPECIAL ARTICLE BY SENATOR OLYMPIA SNOWE: WHY I'M LEAVING THE SENATE

The Washington Post, March 1, 2012

Two truths are all too often overshadowed in today's political discourse: Public service is a most honorable pursuit, and so is bipartisanship.

I have been immeasurably honored to <u>serve the people of Maine</u> for nearly 40 years in public office and for the past 17 years in the United States Senate. It was incredibly difficult to decide that <u>I would not seek a fourth term in the Senate</u>.

Some people were surprised by my conclusion, yet I have spoken on the floor of the Senate for years about the dysfunction and political polarization in the institution. Simply put, the Senate is not living up to what the Founding Fathers envisioned.

During the Federal Convention of 1787, James Madison wrote in his Notes of Debates that "the use of the Senate is to consist in its proceedings with more coolness, with more system, and with more wisdom, than the popular branch." Indeed, the Founding Fathers intended the Senate to serve as an institutional check that ensures all voices are heard and considered, because while our constitutional democracy is premised on majority rule, it is also grounded in a commitment to minority rights.

Yet more than 200 years later, the greatest deliberative body in history is not living up to its billing. The Senate of today routinely jettisons regular order, as evidenced by the body's failure to pass a budget for more than

1,000 days; serially legislates by political brinkmanship, as demonstrated by the debt-ceiling debacle of August that should have been addressed the previous January; and habitually eschews full debate and an open amendment process in favor of competing, up-or-down, take-it-or-leave-it proposals. We witnessed this again in December with votes on two separate proposals for a balanced-budget amendment to the Constitution.

As Ronald Brownstein recently observed in National Journal, Congress is becoming more like a parliamentary system — where everyone simply votes with their party and those in charge employ every possible tactic to block the other side. But that is not what America is all about, and it's not what the Founders intended. In fact, the Senate's requirement of a supermajority to pass significant legislation encourages its members to work in a bipartisan fashion.

One difficulty in making the Senate work the way it was intended is that America's electorate is increasingly divided into red and blue states, with lawmakers representing just one color or the other. Before the 1994 election, 34 senators came from states that voted for a presidential nominee of the opposing party. That number has dropped to just 25 senators in 2012. The result is that there is no practical incentive for 75 percent of the senators to work across party lines.

The great challenge is to create a system that gives our elected officials reasons to look past their differences and find common ground if their initial party positions fail to garner sufficient support. In a politically diverse nation, only by finding that common ground can we achieve results for the common good. That is not happening today and, frankly, I do not see it happening in the near future.

For change to occur, our leaders must understand that there is not only strength in compromise, courage in conciliation and honor in consensus-building — but also a political reward for following these tenets. That reward will be real only if the people demonstrate their desire for politicians to come together after the planks in their respective party platforms do not prevail.

I certainly don't have all the answers, and reversing the corrosive trend of winner-take-all politics will take time. But as I enter a new chapter in my life, I see a critical need to engender public support for the political center, for our democracy to flourish and to find solutions that unite rather than divide us.

I do not believe that, in the near term, the Senate can correct itself from within. It is by nature a political entity and, therefore, there must be a benefit to working across the aisle.

But whenever Americans have set our minds to tackling enormous problems, we have met with tremendous success. And I am convinced that, if the people of our nation raise their collective voices, we can effect a renewal of the art of legislating — and restore the luster of a Senate that still has the potential of achieving monumental solutions to our nation's most urgent challenges. I look forward to helping the country raise those voices to support the Senate returning to its deserved status and stature — but from outside the institution.

Appendix X

SPECIAL ARTICLE BY SUSAN COLLINS:
YES, THE POLITICAL CENTER CAN BE SAVED

Washington Post, March 8, 2012

The recent <u>retirement announcement by Sen. Olympia Snowe</u> is a disappointment to the people of Maine and to me personally. Olympia has devoted her life to public service, and her decision to abandon a race that she surely would have won speaks volumes about the dysfunction in Congress. It has also prompted many people to ask me whether moderates have a future in the Senate.

Olympia will join the pantheon of great leaders our state has produced — Margaret Chase Smith, Bill Cohen, Ed Muskie, George Mitchell. These committed public servants understood that they were sent to Washington to solve problems, not to score political points.

But this is no longer the Senate of Smith and Muskie, of Cohen and Mitchell, and soon it will no longer be the Senate of Olympia Snowe. The change is particularly troubling in these perilous times. With a $15 trillion debt, 13 million people unemployed, oil near $110 per barrel and turmoil throughout the Middle East, there is an urgent need for leaders from the sensible center who realize that neither party has a monopoly on good ideas. The challenges we face will not be met by those who believe compromise is a dirty word.

What has been lost in recent times is a commitment to Congress as an institution, a sense that we are collectively responsible for addressing the issues that confront our country, and that if the institution fails to perform each of us bears responsibility. Just when we most need to function as a team, it appears many of us are unable to see beyond our individual self-interest or the interest of our political party.

When I was a freshman, Sen. John Chafee of Rhode Island, as fine a gentleman as has ever graced the Senate, advised me never to campaign against those with whom I serve. The Senate is too small a place for that, he counseled. Campaign for your fellow Republicans and go to states with open seats, but do not campaign against your Democratic colleagues. It will poison your relationship with them, he warned.

Most senators no longer follow the "Chafee rule." And, yes, hyperbolic — even vitriolic — campaign rhetoric poisons relationships and makes it more difficult for Republicans and Democrats to work together.

If I had to compress all that has gone wrong in one phrase, it would be "perpetual campaign." The gridlock in Congress and the hyperpartisan attacks that fill the Internet reflect a politics unworthy of the American people.

The increasing polarization that has prompted centrists in both parties to depart has convinced me that the center will hold only if we put the same effort into unity that partisans put into division. Predictions of a disappearing political center are a warning of a bleak future that we can avoid only by adhering to our nation's founding principles. Yet I remain confident that principled, common-sense solutions will never go out of style and that the American people still expect government to make real progress on the issues that matter.

Indeed, there are flickerings of bipartisanship that may pull the Senate back from the brink. The "Gang of Six," which sought last year to produce a bipartisan plan to address the debt, attracted more than 40 senators to a meeting where, one after another, senators stood up and announced that they were prepared to compromise and to take the political heat in order to deal with our unprecedented debt. It was encouraging that this group — with nearly equal numbers from each party — included not just moderates, who usually can be counted on to forge coalitions, but liberals and conservatives as well.

More recently, a bipartisan group of senators convened to discuss energy policy and committed to putting together a real plan for our country.

Just last week, <u>Republican Lamar Alexander and Democrat Mark Pryor organized a debate on the Senate floor</u> in which we urged our leaders to consider each appropriations bill in a way that would help restore public confidence, lead to more carefully considered legislation and restore the Senate tradition of free and open debate. Congress must avoid the spectacle of once again missing the deadline for approving spending legislation, which ultimately produces bills that are thousands of pages, while members are left with insufficient time to scrutinize their fine print and trillions in spending.

The rise of the independent voter (<u>40 percent of Americans</u>, according to Gallup) signals a deep dissatisfaction with both parties. The wide electoral swings of recent years suggest that voters have lost patience with candidates who run as pragmatists but then govern as partisans. These trends, and the embryonic signs of bipartisanship in the Senate, give me confidence that the political center will reemerge. That is, after all, where most Americans are.

Acknowledgements

----·•·----

As other authors have recognized, any book is the collective work of untold people who have contributed ideas, knowledge, insights, and recollections. An immense debt is owed to those who have researched and written extensively about U.S. foreign policy, the Clinton impeachment saga, 9/11, the wars in Iraq and Afghanistan, and our national defense and domestic programs.

This book builds on a prior one, *Misuse of Power*, co-authored with Ed Asner in 2005. Much has happened since then and only one chapter remains largely intact. Ed was formerly president of the Screen Actors Guild. In addition to his countless acting roles in television and films, he has been a writer, producer and political activist. He is a contributor to this book.

The discerning moderate Republican responsible for the two quotes in the book is Jill Buzzeo. She is formerly a co-founder and executive of an investment firm and eventually switched her party affiliation to an Independent. She wrote these quotes as part of a letter to a Republican friend just before a presidential election.

I am indebted also to Emeritus Professor of Political Science, Ellis West, at the University of Richmond. His course on the American System of Government stimulated my thinking and he provided insightful comments on the highlight section of the book.

Our patient editor was Molly Kitterick of The Word Process. Besides skillful editing, she asked good questions and became an advisor. A book author should be so lucky.